COOK MEMORIAL PUBLIC LIBRARY DISTRICT

3 1122 00642 2666

P9-CQR-231

J 808.824 SUR   OCT 3   2000
Surface, Mary Hall.
Short scenes and monologues
 for middle school actors

DATE DUE

JAN 3 1 2001	DEC 1 5 2006
JUN 1 0 2001	JAN - 6 2007
	FEB - 8 2007
OCT 19 2001	
DEC 1 0 2001	MAY 3 1 2007
	OCT 1 5 2007
MAR 0 5 2002	
JUL 2 6 2002	
JUL 2 7 2004	
SEP 2 4 2004	
12·23·04	
NOV 1 6 2005	
	RENEWALS
SEP - 5 2006	362-0438

The Library Store   #47-0106

Short Scenes
and Monologues
for Middle School Actors

Smith and Kraus, Inc.
Plays, Monologues, and Scenes for Grades 7–12

Most Valuable Player and Four Other All-Star Plays for Middle and High School Audiences

New Plays from A.C.T.'s Young Conservatory, Volume I

New Plays from A.C.T.'s Young Conservatory, Volume II

New Plays from A.C.T.'s Young Conservatory, Volume III

Tim Mason: Ten Plays from the Minneapolis Children's Theatre

Plays of America from American Folklore for Grades 7–12

Seattle Children's Theatre: Six Plays for Young Audiences Volume I

Seattle Children's Theatre: Six Plays for Young Audiences Volume II

Short Plays for Young Actors

Villeggiatura Trilogy, Condensed for Young Actors

Great Monologues for Young Actors, Volume I

Great Monologues for Young Actors, Volume II

Great Scenes for Young Actors, Volume I

Great Scenes for Young Actors, Volume II

Short Scenes and Monologues for Middle School Actors

Multicultural Monologues for Young Actors

Multicultural Scenes for Young Actors

The Ultimate Play Index for Young Actors Grades 6–12

If you require prepublication information about upcoming Smith and Kraus books, you may receive our semiannual catalogue, free of charge, by sending your name and address to *Smith and Kraus Catalogue, 4 Lower Mill Road, North Stratford, NH 03590. Or call us at (800) 895-4331, fax (603) 643-1831. WWW.SmithKraus.com.*

Short Scenes and Monologues for Middle School Actors

by Mary Hall Surface

YOUNG ACTORS SERIES

A Smith and Kraus Book

COOK MEMORIAL LIBRARY
413 N. MILWAUKEE AVE.
LIBERTYVILLE, IL 60048
OCT 3 2000

Dedicated to Malinda
who one day
will be in middle school.

MHS

A Smith and Kraus Book
Published by Smith and Kraus, Inc.
PO Box 127, Lyme, NH 03768
(800) 895-4331
www.SmithKraus.com

Copyright ©1999 by Mary Hall Surface
All rights reserved
Manufactured in the United States of America
First Edition: December 1999
10 9 8 7 6 5 4 3 2 1

CAUTION: The material in this book is fully protected under the copyright laws of the United States of America, and of all countries covered by the International Copyright Union (including the Dominion of Canada and the rest of the British Commonwealth), and of all countries covered by the Pan-American Copyright Convention and the Universal Copyright Convention, and of all countries with which the United States has reciprocal copyright relations. All rights, including professional, amateur, motion picture, recitation, lecturing, public reading, radio broadcasting, television, video or sound taping, all other forms of mechanical or electronic reproductions such as CD-ROM and CD-I, information storage and retrieval systems and photocopying, and the rights of translation into foreign languages, are strictly reserved. Please refer to bibliographical information for performance rights.

Book design by Julia Hill Gignoux, Freedom Hill Design

The Library of Congress Cataloging-In-Publication Data
Surface, Mary Hall.
Short scenes and monologues for middle school actors / by Mary Hall Surface. —1st ed.
        p. cm. — (Young actors series)
        Includes bibliographical references.
    Summary: A collection of original scenes and monologues
        written expecially for middle-school actors.
                ISBN 1-57525-179-5
    1. Monologues — Juvenile literature. 2. Dialogues — Juvenile literature.
3. Acting — Juvenile literature. [1. Acting. 2. Monologues] I. Young actors series
                PN2080.S87   1999
            812'.5408—dc21   99-052457

Contents

Introduction

No longer a child, but not yet a teenager, the middle school actor needs monologues and scenes that speak directly to them — that capture their everyday but gigantically important struggles with school, friends, and parties, as well as their painful wrestlings with the hard knocks and hard choices of adolescence. In my twenty years of working for and with young people as a director, playwright, and teacher, I have found that eleven- to fourteen-year-olds bring unrivaled energy to the work of making theatre. One minute they are devoted performers. The next minute they are infuriating clowns. The next they are ricocheting off the walls simply because they are twelve. Most often, they just want your serious attention.

I have written this book to share material that works with this age group. All of the pieces have been at the core of my middle school acting curriculum in inner-city, suburban, and rural schools; many of the pieces are from my plays, which have been widely performed on amateur and professional stages. I have tried to present the material in a form that drama teachers across the United States have requested — short monologues with clear emotional turning points and transitions, short scenes for two and four actors with strong relationships and specific objectives, and short scenes for multiple actors in which the roles have relatively equal weight.

In the monologues, my goal is to give young actors a chance to be in a specific dramatic moment. The character in the monologue wants something from his or her unseen partner. For example, they want their mother's approval; they want to find something out; they want to stop hurting.

What the character will do to get what he or she wants is what drives the monologue. Too many monologues are story-driven, in past tense, and overly narrative. But what young actors need to do on stage is build relationships with other characters, react to what is happening *now,* and work to get what they want. These monologues set up clear imaginary circumstances for that work. Their strong emotional turning points and transitions demand that the actor explore a range of emotions, even within a short monologue form.

In the scenes, I want young actors to clearly envision the imaginary circumstances of the scene, to behave truthfully within those circumstances, and to pursue what their character wants as actively as possible. Many of the scenes set up compelling physical circumstances — riding on a Ferris wheel, tug-o-warring with sheets, climbing to the edge of a rocky ledge, being a pawn in a giant, frightening board game, or building a railroad. This is to push young actors to realize that the development of the physical life of a scene and a character is of equal importance to "saying the lines." Indeed, some very important story moments in the scenes are wordless. Also, the text of the scenes is designed to encourage young actors to look beyond spoken lines to the subtext — to what the characters are thinking and feeling "beneath" the words. And the text is filled with images — images that the actor must see exactly in order to give a character full three-dimensional life. When you understand all that is inside a character, then you know "how to say the line."

The middle schooler is not a simple creature. So the subject matter I have chosen for these monologues and scenes is as diverse as they are. Much of it is rooted in their everyday world — a world that is multicultural, complex, funny, and frightening. I have also included material based in history and some that crosses into an imaginary realm. I include this material because it is so appealing to actors in this age group. As importantly, it stretches the young actor to develop nonhuman characters, to imagine themselves to be older (a practice I do not advocate in realistic material), or to stand in someone else's shoes in another place and time.

I hope this collection will encourage young actors to make clear, strong choices; to develop characters with vivid physical, emotional and vocal ranges; to build rich, powerful relationships on stage; and to use all their creativity to imagine ways to tell the big stories in these short pieces.

Mary Hall Surface
Washington, D.C.
July 1999

CHAPTER ONE
Monologues for Young Women

Ellie

(Talking to her Dad.)

ELLIE: Please, Dad, it doesn't cost that much. It's the coolest thing. It's a set — twenty different nail polish colors and matching tattoos. Of course they come off! Look, I'll make up my bed. Promise. Take the garbage out twice a day. Never be late for the bus. And Karla and I will never fight again when she comes over, because now I'll be Karla's best friend instead of Tracy because now I'll have the best stuff. *(Pause.)* Didn't you know that's why she comes over? That's why anybody comes over. If you've got good stuff, you've got friends.

Maureen

(Talking to her best friend, Shay.)

MAUREEN: How's this? "So, Dylan, I'm having a Halloween party on Friday. Wanna come?" No way. I'd faint. He'd run! OK, how 'bout this: "So, Dylan. Stop by my house on Friday. Maybe I'll be having a party or something…maybe." And maybe the earth will open up and swallow me! Oh Shay, I might as well face it. I just don't know how to say, "I like you, Dylan. For over a year. I know we're just friends, but I'd like to be more." I said it. I just *said* it! Where's the phone?!

Sally

(Talking to her Grandmother ["Abuela" in Spanish] who is leaving to live in a nursing home.)

SALLY: I've finished, Abuela. I put your things in this suitcase. It's not too heavy. See? Your little china dog — I wrapped it in newspaper so it won't break. You can put it on the shelf by the window in your new room. Nursing homes have windows. Sure they do. You can look out. Remember how you used to show me pictures in the clouds? Of hats, and dogs and... Don't you remember, Abuela? Abuela! It's me. Sally. "Sally Sue and her quacking quacker-oo?" Don't you remember *me? (Pause.)* Vamanos, Abuela. Dad's waiting.

Aury

(Talking to her Mom.)

AURY: I'm not going back to that camp, Mom. You can't make me. I told you what happened! We were on the bus to go swimming. Kalila and I were talking. Then this kid behind me taps me on the shoulder and asks, "Were you adopted?" I said, "No!" He says, "But weren't you raised by white people? You don't talk like us." I tried to defend myself. I made some smart remark, but they just made fun of me. They've been asking me questions like that all summer! Why do they have to tease me? I feel like I'm not black enough for them…or for me.

Chase

(Talking to a new friend.)

CHASE: Look, I like being a tomboy. I like to play sports. And I like to wear these jeans and this shirt. So what's the problem? My Dad understands. He thinks it's OK for me to have boys as friends. But my Mom, she drives me nuts!! Like the other night, we were at the dinner table, when the phone rings. Mom gets it, then I hear her say, "Chase, it's a boy." Then all my brothers, even my father, break out into this chorus of "Oooooos." "A guy, Chase, Oooooo." "Is it your boyfriend, Chase? Oooo." I mean, come on! I've always had guys as friends. Why do they have to tease me like that? Except...I don't think Mom is teasing. She wants me to have a boyfriend so I'll be more of a girl. I wish she would just leave me alone! *(Pause.)* But she's right. I do want a guy to like me for more than being...one of the guys. I just don't think it will ever happen.

Karina

(Talking to a rather eccentric girl she has just met.)

KARINA: You wanna know why I never talk? Because people don't listen to what I say. Sure, it hurts to be left out of all the games or the boyfriend talk. Not much I could say about boyfriends even if I was left *in*. The only guy who ever asked me to go with him — when he asked me, I said, "Go where?" But hey, I'm used to being left out. But, see, that never happens to you. Cause you're the kind of weird that people think is interesting. I'm just weird. *(Thoughtfully.)* Isn't it weird being weird? You know...we could be weird together. That sounded weird. What I mean is...friends. Wanna come over after school?

Elena

(Talking to her best friend, Roberto, whose wealthy parents are hosting a Christmas party.)

ELENA: How do you *think* I feel? You're lying to me, Roberto! You tell me to meet you here — that we'll go to your Christmas party, and now you say: "My mother is sick. There's not going to be any party." I don't believe you! You're mother's not sick. You just don't want me to come. You never really wanted me to come. You were just making fun of me! *(Throwing down a small bundle.)* Here. These are oranges I picked from my garden. I hope you and your parents enjoy them at your party! Why would I want to be with a bunch of rich people anyway! *(Pause.)* I thought you were my friend. We were going to do the play for everyone that we practiced. I put on my best dress, see? Why can't I come?

Mia

(Talking to her drama teacher.)

MIA: Please, Mrs. Duarte. Don't cast me as the kid! I always have to play the kid. But I can play anything! Watch. I can be a Mom: "Oh honey, welcome home from school. Here are some cookies I just baked for you." Or a real Mom: "Hey honey, jump in, bus is leaving, brought you a snack, how was school, did we lose your brother?" Or wait. A dog. I love playing dogs. "Yip. Yip. Yip. Where's my ball? Just let me play catch. I love to play catch." Or a villain: "Give me the money, and give me it now! No questions and nobody'll get hurt." See! I have great range! *(Pause.)* It's just…I'm the littlest in everything. Nobody ever gives me a chance… in anything. Please. Just let me try.

Lep

(Talking to a classmate.)

LEP: Listen, please. I want you to understand! I don't remember much before I was five. I know we lived in many different camps. Refugee camps. But I do remember the night that everything changed. We were sleeping, my sister and I. We could hear footsteps coming closer to our tent. We'd heard footsteps before, but they'd never stopped for us. Then a man, with a clean face and shiny glasses, handed us two airline tickets. He said, "You're coming to the United States." And then he gave me a little American flag. I thought it was a toy, so I played with it, and my sister shined the embassy man's flashlight on it, like a spotlight. It was so small. So beautiful. That one little flag held all my hopes. How could I ever say anything bad about this country? It still holds my dreams. Maybe not yours, but *mine*.

Lindsey

(Talking to her friend.)

LINDSEY: I had a boyfriend when I was five. Why can't I get one now? I had them lining up! In kindergarten, I got married. It was just pretend, but we kissed and walked all the way to the circle-time spot holding hands. Then in first grade, three boys all wanted to marry me at once. I was adored! What happened? *(Pause.)* Maybe I don't deserve a boyfriend now. Back then I was little and cute and smart. Now I'm the tallest girl in my state. People think I'm twenty, but I'm thirteen. You don't get glasses, braces, and pimples all in the same month unless you're thirteen. Oh, I wish I could snap my fingers and the right-now-ugly me would just disappear! Then I'd be the next me — whoever that is. Who do you think I'll be when being thirteen is over?

Lilly

(Talking to her teacher. It is 1943, during World War II.)

LILLY: I heard him! I heard President Roosevelt on the radio. He said every American who has a scrap of land should plant a victory garden. If we grow our own food, then the big farmers can send the food they grow to the soldiers. That'll help us win the war, won't it? My yard's only five by five from back porch to alley. But Momma says I can plant beans, maybe some squash. It won't be much, but I know it'll help. It's gotta help. I'll do anything! Cause…my brother's over there. In Germany or somewhere. We used to get letters from him, but we haven't gotten one in a long time. I get so scared every time I see a car comin' down the road. That's how you find out. A man in a uniform brings you a telegram if…I can't think about it. I'm gonna plant every patch a' dirt I can. What do I do first?

Kara

(Talking to her Mother.)

KARA: What business? What business is it of mine that you drink yourself stupid almost every night? It's my life, too, Mom. I can't bring anybody here. Because I never know what you might say to one of my friends. I can't have a party. I can't do anything like a normal kid because my Mom's a drunk! *(Pause, as she sees her Mother begin to cry.)* Mom. Oh, Mom. Don't cry. I'm sorry. Have you had a really bad week at work? Let me get you something to eat. A sandwich? Or some chips? I'll get you anything. I'll do anything...to make you better. Please, Mom. I need you. Don't do this anymore. Please.

Tasha

(Talking to her Mother.)

TASHA: Why does Uncle Zeke have to move, Momma? I know he got a good job, with *(Quoting the adults.)* "lots of opportunity." But it's Kwanzaa! We're supposed to be together to honor our families and celebrate our ancestors. And Uncle Zeke's my favorite ancestor — dead or alive! You know what he told me? He said I was one in a long line of great black musicians. Famous ones, who used to play in fancy clubs right here in our neighborhood a long time ago. He said if I keep practicin' my piano, I can be as famous as Jelly Roll Morton. Call myself "Cinnamon Bun." *(Laughing.)* He says the best things. *(Pause.)* You think he left because I wasn't practicin' hard enough? I was tryin', really I was. Oh, Momma! Maybe I can catch him. He just left! *(She runs to the door and stops.)* He's gone.

Shelly

(Talking to her friend, Clara.)

SHELLY: It was weird, Clara. Here we were on this great class trip, and I couldn't see anything. We were in the art gallery. I knew we were supposed to be looking at the paintings. I had my sketchbook, and I tried to sketch some of the figures, but all I could see was me — me standing there looking. It's like there's a camera outside my body, and it's always playing the film of my life in my head. I try to turn it off, or at least change the channel! But in my head, it's always playing. It's not like I think I'm so great that I deserve a movie about me. Right! Who'd come to see it? It's more like I'm watching my life, waiting to see what's going to happen next. Does that ever happen to you?

Alana

(Talking to her friend.)

ALANA: You start with just little lies. Like goin' out to the store without askin'. Or steppin' out with somebody, but tellin' your Momma you're at church. She wouldn't have known, but my old nosy neighbor lady's always sittin' on her porch. Always in my business. Why's she have to watch me every time I come and go? Callin' the police, sayin' we're makin' too much noise on the corner. Me and my girlfriends, we weren't doin' nothin'! She don't call the police when the boys are out there. No, she's too scared to do that, but she'll call 'em on us. She's just lookin' to feel some power. *(Laughs a little.)* Power. That's what lies give you, too. Where else in this world am I ever gonna get any power? Can you tell me that? I got me a secret world. Nobody is takin' that from me. Nobody!!

Jennifer

(Talking to her friend.)

JENNIFER: What do you think of my plan? This really big piece of material *(Showing her friend.)* is for the hallway mirror. And this lacey one *(Showing her.)* will cover the mirror in the dining room. In my room, it was easy. I just took the mirror off the wall. I haven't figured out what to do in the bathroom yet. That mirror is huge and my least favorite. Maybe I could accidentally break it. No wait, that's bad luck, isn't it? Who cares. How could my luck get any worse! I look like *me* and my sister could win every beauty contest in the universe. I don't ever want to look at myself next to her again. So I'll just make all the mirrors in the house disappear. You think Mom will mind?

Jasmine

(Talking to her little sister.)

JASMINE: You gonna let them tell you that? Then you are no little sister of mine. Sure, if you listen to some folks, yeah, our chances are crummy. You look in the newspaper, and it'll say we're not supposed to graduate high school without a baby, that someone in our family is on drugs, two others are locked up, and we all got an abusive, hustling boyfriend. But that, sister, is not the story the newspapers will write about me. Not today or ever! My mind is set. I can achieve. I'm not gettin' stuck in anybody's profile because I have potential! Look into my eyes. Do you see it, little sister? It's my fire. Mark my words. I am gonna be somebody. You need to make up your mind if you're gonna be somebody, too.

Meg

(Talking to a friend who has just rejected her.)

MEG: Sure, I'm a clown! I'm a joke a minute! No, Gina, wait! Don't turn away, too. I wanna explain! See...I used to have a great group of friends. We did everything together. But something changed. I don't know what I did, or what I said. But one day I walked up to my friends in front of school. They were laughing and talking like we always did. But they were standing in this tight little circle, and when I tried to stand next to somebody, they wouldn't let me in. They didn't really push me out. They just wouldn't let me in. I thought maybe they were playing or something, so I started to laugh. But they weren't playing. I wanted to cry, but instead...I just kept laughing. I've tried to keep laughing ever since. Now do you understand?

Franny

(Talking to her friend.)

FRANNY: What if I had all the money in the world? That's easy. Bet you think I'm gonna say, "Buy a sports car," cause I like your brother's so much. But what would I do? Look at it? I can't drive yet. Maybe you think I'll say, "A trip to Tahiti or Hawaii!" But you know my parents. They won't let me go around the block by myself, much less to Hawaii. No. I would spend my money on *(Big dramatic pause.)* facial surgery. Sure! They can make you look like the magazine models. If you don't like your nose, they change it. Or your chin? Well, *(Making the motion of a magic wand.)* Zing! You get a new one. Me? I'd have a total remake. Then all my problems would be over. Zing!

Nannerl

(Talking to her brother, Wolfgang Mozart, in 1762.)

NANNERL: "Momma, I don't think I want to perform tomorrow. I'd rather just watch." That's what I said to her, Wolfgang. You were there! Or were you so lost in your music that you didn't hear me! Maybe you'll miss me when I'm no longer next to you. We've always performed together. Me singing and you at the harpsichord. Remember our concerts in Munich? They were so beautiful! But that was before. Before Poppa began to see only you. To hear only you. "Wolfgang Amadeus Mozart." "The most talented child in the world!" Why must I be forgotten? I can compose. I play four instruments, just like you. Is it because I am the *sister*, and not the *brother*? I don't understand. Is your light so bright that I can no longer even stand in your shadow? Wolfy, please. I just want us to be happy. To be a family! Wolfy, why won't you answer me?!

CHAPTER TWO

Monologues for Young Men

Corey

(Talking to his friend.)

COREY: You know your problem? You have no imagination. If it was up to you, every day of your life would be exactly the same. Not me! I'm an adventurer. You know what I'm gonna do? One day I'm not getting off at our subway stop. I'm gonna keep going. To the end of the line. Then catch another train, and another one, till I get where I wanna go. I'm sure I'll know it when I get there. I can see it. The greatest place on earth. *(Pause.)* It's gotta be out there somewhere. I sure haven't seen it around here. Have you?

Roberto

(Talking to his best friend, Elena.)

ROBERTO: Your Mom has to work? On Christmas Day? That's crazy! Nobody works on Christmas! Bus drivers, maybe. And taxi drivers. And, OK, the people who work in stores that never close — all right! So, lots of people work on Christmas! But your Mom shouldn't have to! Here's a plan. She tells the Hendrick's, "You're just gonna mess up your big ole house anyway opening all your presents. I'll come clean the next day." What do you think? Elena, don't look so sad. You won't be by yourself on Christmas. I'll think of something. Promise.

Yuri

(Talking to his Father.)

YURI: Look, Dad. I'm sorry. But you don't know what it's like! What if your boss walked into your office every morning and yelled at you through a bullhorn! That's what Mr. Morton does. Robert said *his* assistant principal doesn't use a bullhorn to get the kids into class. It's insulting! Then today, he comes on the intercom and says: "You people have been so good you get next Monday off." It's a national holiday! Every kid in America has Monday off from school. He must think we're morons! If he didn't treat us like dumb animals, maybe we wouldn't act like... *(Realizing he has behaved badly.)* like dumb animals. *(Pause.)* I didn't actually *break* the bullhorn. I just hid it. Probably forever. I'm sorry.

Brian

(Talking to his Grandmother.)

BRIAN: How come you go around braggin' about me to all your friends, but then you say to me: "You gotta do better, you gotta do better." What do you want? Grades don't get any better than mine. I play sports. I go to...*sometimes* I go to church. Now Grandmomma, don't get on me about that. I go! Just not twelve times a week like you do. I got other things goin'. Friends. Plans. Stuff to do. *(Pause.)* Ah, Grandmomma, don't get that sad look. I'm not goin' down any wrong road. You taught me better than that. But how about braggin' about me to *me* sometime? All right?

Bernie

(Talking to his Father.)

BERNIE: Dad, if you'd let me explain then you'll understand! See, I'm spending the night at David's house. There's gonna be a ring around the moon Friday night. It's an astronomical phenomenon! We get extra credit if we stay up late to see it. You can't see a once-in-a-lifetime thing like this by yourself! Don't look worried. I promise, we won't do any of the things we did last time. No bike riding after dark, no chemistry experiments in the kitchen. Just moon watching...with your binoculars. Please, can I borrow them, Dad, please???

Jamal

(Talking to a kid who is looking to cause trouble at JAMAL's neighborhood park.)

JAMAL: Why you wanna come in here and start somethin'? Walkin' in here, bumpin' into people when you walk past. What're you hopin' is gonna happen? That somebody's gonna take you on? Start a big fight? Make you feel big? Well, you must not know the rule. We only got one big rule on this playground, for all those little kids over there, and for us on the court. No disrespect. From anybody. We respect one another. And anybody who comes in here does the same. So you either play by our rule, or you're out. What's it gonna be?

Alex

(Talking to his Father as they enter a museum exhibition.)

ALEX: Dad, I told you, I'm not interested in this stuff! You're always doin' this. Draggin' me to museums to see a bunch of old things right in the middle of baseball on TV — *(He sees airplane.)* Wow! Is that Lindbergh's plane? The real plane that he flew across the ocean in? I bet it's a fake. *(Reading the airplane's name.)* "The Spirit of St. Louis." It *is* the real plane. But it's so small. Man, Lindbergh must have been one brave pilot. He flew all that way in something built like that? And he was the first! Incredible! Dad, you should've brought me here before. What kind of a Dad are you?

Eddie

(Talking to his friend, Reuben.)

EDDIE: I've got the greatest idea. What if we took over the White House. Not the whole place, just the thermostat. Think of the power! In the middle of some high-level negotiations between heads of state, we could turn the place into an igloo. They'd be calling the Secret Service for sweaters and scarves. Nobody could sign any treaties because their fingers would be frozen together. Or get this: It's summer. The President is having a fancy party for a million guests, and we pump the place to 110 degrees. "All points bulletin. Find the thermostat villains." Finally, we'd bust out and demand... *(EDDIE hasn't thought about this.)* something. What would we ask for? World peace? Uh, no more pollution? Wait. I got it. Year-round professional football! On demand! What, you don't think this'll work?

Conner

(Talking to his Mother.)

CONNER: Mom. I gotta stay home today. See? Look at my eyes. They're all hazy-looking. *(Taking a step back.)* You don't have to feel me! I already took my temperature. It's bad. Really bad. You go ahead and go to work. I'll be fine — not *fine,* I'm sick! But you can leave. It's OK. Don't give me that look! It's your "I don't believe you look." I told you. I don't feel like going to school. *That* is the truth. Nobody will notice I'm absent, so what does it matter? If I fell off the earth it wouldn't matter to anybody in the whole school. Wait, Mom, are you calling the doctor? OK. OK. Where's my backpack?

Ty

(He is talking to a former friend.)

TY: You think I'm like a sheep or something? I don't walk off a cliff just because you tell me to. I got more brains in my head than that! What you gotta do right now is tell me where my sister is. She told me she'd meet me here, so where is she?! Did you lie to her? Did you tell her I was messin' around with you and your crew? If you did... Listen, I'm not hangin' with you any more. I'm out. My sister's out, too. We want something better than what you've got to offer. I'm not spending my life gettin' into trouble. You better tell me, now, where is she?!! I'm not afraid of you. I'll call the police so quick you won't be able to run fast enough to get away.

Chris

(Talking to his Father.)

CHRIS: Dad, I like baseball. Really. I've played it since I was six. Remember? You called me your six-year-old slugger. Well, I'm twelve now, and I've just got other things I wanna do after school. No big deal. Dad, why are looking at me like that? I didn't ask if I could dye my hair blue, I just wanna quit the team. Don't look so disappointed. We can still play. You and me, on Saturdays. But no pickup games at the park, or with anybody, OK? I don't want to hear it anymore: "Move in everybody. Chris is up to bat. Easy out. Easy out." Please, Dad, I can't stay on the team. Don't make me.

Matt

(Talking to his friend.)

MATT: You want to *stay* here? Not me. It's the worst thing I can think of! Being stuck in middle school for the rest of my life? What a nightmare! Picture this. I'm twenty-three. I've been trying to pass an algebra test for ten years, but every time I take it, I fail! And when my history project is due, I've lost it, for the twentieth time! I'm taller than everybody else. Hey, that might not be bad. Still, I bet no one would notice me. Finally I try to escape, but the doors are all locked! Sirens go off, and over the intercom I hear "Matt is trying to graduate. Matt is trying to graduate. Stop him! Capture him!" So I run and run until they corner me in the cafeteria. I pelt the principal with french fries. Then they make me sit in detention until I'm forty! No, I'm headin' for high school the minute they'll let me. Life's gotta be easier there.

Jason

(JASON has just knocked over a vase. He is talking to his Mother.)

JASON: Mom, it was an accident, I swear! I wasn't running! I was hurrying. And the table must have been sticking out in the hallway more than it usually does, cause I run — *hurry* past this vase every day and I've never broken it before! I'm sorry. Can I glue it back together? I'm great at puzzles! *(He looks at the million pieces.)* I guess not. Mom, it's my feet. They've got a life of their own. They're huge. Uncontrollable. Like an alien life form! You know the new boots you bought me last week? They don't fit anymore! And the new gloves, too. It's like my hands are three times too big for my arms. Maybe I should join the circus. People could pay money to see the kid with the weirdest body on earth. *(Using a ringmaster's voice.)* "Trips on his mother's table without noticing!" I'm really sorry, Mom. I'll do something to fix it. Promise.

John

(JOHN is talking to his aunt's maid, Emma. It is the day after the Japanese bombed Pearl Harbor, 1941.)

JOHN: Where were you when you heard, Emma? I was just sittin' there, playin' Chinese checkers with Warren. Momma had just washed little sister's hair, and had her sittin' on a stool in front of the stove. She was combin', then Daddy says, "Hush up." He had his head up against the radio, close as it would go. Everything got quiet, 'cept for a voice talkin' 'bout a place that sounds almost magic — Pearl Harbor. "Bombing. They're bombing," Daddy said. I ran to the window. Those planes had to be flyin' over our house, 'cause Momma and Daddy seemed so scared. Little Ellen ran, too. She was cryin'. Then Momma says, "Get away from that window. You'll catch your death with wet hair." Then Momma just started combin' again. But it was different. Everything's different. What do you think's gonna happen? To the whole world?

Shane

(Talking to his new classmates.)

SHANE: Tell you something interesting about me?
(Shrugs.) Nothin' to say. I got a sister, two brothers, and I
live in Crestwood. *(Shrugs again.)* I don't know. Maybe
you should ask somebody else. No, hold up. There's one
thing… Nobody I know can do it. Maybe I should make you
guess. *(Laughs a little.)* Nah. Listen. I can ride down a
whole city block on the back wheel of my bike. For real!
You don't believe me? You should see me. I got skill. You
start on the top of a hill. Then once you get goin' you pull
up, and ride on one wheel all the way down. Takes balance.
Endurance. I got all those things. Are those interesting?

Jackie

(Young Jackie Robinson is talking to his brother Mac in 1930.)

JACKIE: Mac, I hear what you and Momma say. *(Quoting his mother and brother.)* "Be patient. Good things will come to good people." But some days I just can't take it! Why, Mac? Why do I have to be stuck up in the balcony when I go to the movies? Why do I have to sit in the back of the bus, even when there're plenty of empty seats up front? I wanna drink out of that water fountain, but I can't, 'cause it's got a sign on it sayin' "Whites Only"? Why can't I go to that nice, pretty school instead of mine? Who made the rule that said I'm worth less than a white kid? It hurts, Mac. Someday, I'm gonna change it. I don't know how, but I'm not livin' in a world like this all my life. I'm gonna change it.

Cortez

(Talking to his Father on the first day of a new school.)

CORTEZ: Poppa! Are you crazy! Put it away. Put the camera away! *(By CORTEZ's reaction, we know his Father has put the camera away.)* Dios Mio, Poppa! You wanna make me look stupid? You see any other kid's father here with a camera? *(Cutting his father off.)* I know, I know. *(Imitating his father.)* "Your uncle in Santa Domingo, your cousins in New York, your old grandpoppy in Santiago, they all want a picture of Cortez on the first day of new school!" What are you, loco? Look, we'll take one when I come home. With Momma. She'll put her arm around me, you'll say "Sonria *[Smile]*," it'll be beautiful. OK? Hey, where're ya goin'? The first bell hasn't rung. If you just wanna hang... I don't mind. *(Pause, as he looks at his new surroundings.)* I don't know anybody at this school. So...why do I care if you take a picture? OK. *(Smiling big.)* Photo op! *(The unseen father flashes the picture as CORTEZ smiles.)* Adios, Poppa. *(CORTEZ turns and walks toward his new school.)*

Clint

(Talking to his best friend, David.)

CLINT: You think it's tough to start eighth grade? Think back, David! Nothing could be worse than the first day of first grade! Picture this: My Mom bursts into tears, which makes me all weird and confused because I think: "Hey, I'm six. Shouldn't I be the one who's crying?" Then I walk by myself through this big front door. It looks like the entrance to another galaxy. And here comes Mrs. Walsh, our teacher. She trots us around, showing us the art table, and the sand table, and the picture of Charley Chipmunk on the wall. This chipmunk had the first grade rules in little bubbles, like in a comic book, coming out of its mouth. "I am Charley Chipmunk. I am courteous to others. I respect my classmates." While she's doing the grand tour, I keep raising my hand, but she never calls on me. OK, I only raised it this much *(He raises his hand to about rib level.)* but I was petrified! So I never tell her that I have to go to the bathroom! *(Pause.)* Use your imagination about what happened next! Come on, David. Eighth grade can't be any worse. We'll walk in together. Right up those ten thousand steps. It's no big deal. *(With a note of doubt.)* Right?

Alan

(Talking to his little sister, in front of a flower shop.)

ALAN: I know this is the store. See, here's Mom's bus stop. She waits by here every day. These *are* beautiful flowers. She says, "Someday, I'll have the smell of a garden again in my house." We can give her that smell! We have money...a little. These yellow ones can't cost too much. *(He looks at the price.)* Seven dollars. Maybe these. They have much smaller blossoms. *(He looks at the price.)* Six dollars. Why do they cost so much! *(Speaking to the seller.)* Excuse me. Excuse me, sir. Our mother. She is lonely for her country, where they have many flowers. But we live here now. Your flowers could make her happy again. I have for four dollars. What can I buy?

Glaston

(A young storybook hero is talking to a reluctant dragon.)

GLASTON: Tell me another story, Dragon. Of saints and battles, dragons and armor from the olden days! Weren't creatures like you quite plentiful then? Oh, the world must have been filled with thrills and surprises! Tell me! Didn't all the knights from distant lands come together for great tournaments to joust and wrestle? And didn't they wear suits of armor that sparkled in the sun? And didn't they — what? *(He listens, then repeats what the dragon has just told him.)* "Rip and bash themselves up just to prove who was the noblest?" Why, that makes them sound silly. Knights and saints aren't silly. They're heroes! You have it all wrong, Dragon. You've been living underground far too long. Your memory is bad. Let's try again, Dragon. Tell me another story. Dragon!

CHAPTER THREE

Monologues for Young Women or Young Men

Mark / Marcy

(Talking to his/her friend.)

MARK / MARCY: You don't get it, do you? My Mom said no, so stop bugging me! She always says no, every time I ask her. "Who'll take care of it? Who'll take it for walks in the rain and the snow?" I will. I will! But she doesn't believe me. Your Mom's different. You get whatever you want. You're lucky. Wait a minute. Do you really even want a dog? I bet you just want one because I can't have one. You just want to make me miserable! Some best friend.

Alex / Alexis

(Talking to his/her friend.)

ALEX / ALEXIS: Don't worry! Be happy! That's my motto. You always get so worried about every little thing. Like you were so sure you wouldn't score in soccer today, and you did. And you knew you wouldn't pass your geography test, and you got an A! I got a B. I'm the one who should be worried. My Mom said if I got more than one B this quarter, she'd take the phone out of my room. And I've still got that big science project to go. I'll never ace that. And what will I do without my phone? Oh, see what you did! You got me worried. Some friend!

Aaron / Karen

(Talking to his/her friend.)

AARON / KAREN: "Why are you lookin' at me like that?
Because I'm young? And I'm black? Oh, so now you've
found out I go to the *good* school so you got a change of
attitude! Well, I was the same person I was five minutes
ago when you thought I was a nobody!" Man, I wish I'd said
that. Made him feel what it's like! Why can't I just walk
into a room and not have the first thing people notice be
the color of my skin? Is that too much to ask? I am proud
of my color but it's only part of who I am. It's not the whole
me. Why couldn't he see that?

Casey / Casey

(Talking to his/her Mom.)

CASEY / CASEY: OK, Mom. Sign on the dotted line. "I
hereby promise that Casey can have his/her grandmother's
golf clubs." I want a contract! Don't you remember last
week? I said, "Are we going to the mall?" Answer: "Yes,
Casey, tomorrow." Next day: "When are we going to the
mall, Mom?" Answer: "We aren't, Casey. Where ever did
you get that idea?" I'm not saying you lie. Sometimes you
just "forget." This way, there'll be no disagreement. So,
sign here please. Oh, can I borrow your pen? Mom!

Don / Dawn

(Talking to his/her Mother.)

DON / DAWN: What do you think? I'll write an advertisement for a friend, put it in the newspaper, then I can choose from the applicants. How does this sound? "Wanted: One friend, the same age as me, who likes soccer, water parks, and going to the movies." See, I want them to be almost exactly like me, but with a few variations. Wait, there's more: "Must always be home when I call, must think my jokes are funny and that my clothes are the best." I don't think that's unreasonable. *(Pause.)* I do have a last part. But if I put it in, I don't know if anybody will apply. "Will never break a promise. Will never tell secrets." Do you think that's possible for a middle school kid? Mom, tell me what you think!

George / Grace

(Talking to his/her friend.)

GEORGE / GRACE: "Why don't I have my homework? Well, Mr. Starks, to do homework, it seems to me like you've got to have a home. And in my case, 'home' depends on what day of the week it is. Couple of days, I'm at my grandmother's, then I'm with my aunt, and if I'm lucky I get to stay with my Dad once a month. Most days, I don't know which home I'm supposed to go to!" *(Pause.)* I wish that's what I'd said to him. The teacher who tells us we have to hand stuff in on time, then turns it back to us late. Shoot, I wouldn't honor him with the truth of my life. Watch me. I'm gonna rise above him...and everything else.

Terry / Teri

(Talking to his/her Mother.)

TERRY / TERI: You can look at it if you want. I mean, you don't have to. It's not that great. It's just a book I made. Of pictures. Poems. A couple of stories, but they're the worst. Writing stories is my weak area. I know you'll be happy with the grade, Mom. I got an A. Means I aced the quarter. So did Pat. Best friends. Best grades. But I was hoping you could... Never mind. It's not that important. I'll come back when you're off the phone. *(Turns to leave, but then turns back around.)* Would you just read it, Mom? Let me know if it's any good. I want to know from *you*. OK? OK.

Tim / Tara

(Talking to the Mayor.)

TIM / TARA: I'll tell you the worst thing about my neighborhood. We got wild life. You think I'm talking about the kids? No! I'm talking about wild possums. Dogs nobody takes care of. And rats! My grandmother and I were walking home from the grocery and she says, "Look, baby, isn't that cute! A litter of puppies playin' on the corner." But when we got up closer, they were rats, big as hound-dog puppies, climbin' and jumpin' all over each other like they owned the place. My grandmother about had a heart attack. Mr. Mayor, I know I am only thirteen. But you have got to listen. We don't deserve to live like this. Aren't you ashamed?

Sam / Sammy

(Talking to his/her Father.)

SAM / SAMMY: I just did it once, Dad. What's the big deal? You used to smoke. I've seen pictures. You and Uncle Dave sittin' around in the back yard smokin'. And you smoked a cigar when Camren was born. I saw you. And you smoked another one when you got your new job. And cigars are gross! I just smoked one little cigarette — half smoked. So why are you jumping all over me? I just did it because...I wanted to. You know. To check it out. And... OK, Eric / Ann asked me to. I gotta do what Eric / Ann asks me to do. How else am I gonna be his / her friend?

Jim / Jean

(Talking to his/her teacher.)

JIM / JEAN: Respect is a two-way street. Why should I respect anybody who treats me like that? All I was doin' was sittin' on the bus, listenin' to my music, lookin' out the window. OK, my backpack was on the seat next to me, but there were only four people on the whole bus. Then this old guy gets on, walks up, and pushes my backpack on the floor. He didn't poke me to get my attention, ask me, nothin'. Just pushed my backpack on that dirty floor. Then he didn't even sit in the seat next to me. I mean, what's that about? He shoved it on the floor cause I'm a kid. That's all. Do I deserve that? Like I say, respect is a two-way street. He's got to be respecting me, if he wants the same.

Cat

(An enchanted CAT is talking to the Sorcerer's apprentice. Klaus, the apprentice who has mastered only a few magic spells, is lazing around the Sorcerer's workshop.)

CAT: Learning another useful spell I see! Klaus, how can you be so lazy? You've only begun to know the power of the Sorcerer's magic. Why, you could learn to change a chair into a horse that you could ride into the village. Or change yourself into a fox and race as fast as lightning through the trees. Or you could soar like a eagle through the sky! *(KLAUS ignores the CAT.)* Klaus, are you listening? Please! You *must* be curious about the Sorcerer's spells. Where do you think he goes when he leaves the workshop? What do you think he does? He might be — *(The CAT is prevented from speaking, as if he/she is under a spell.)* He might be...a good Sorcerer who does only good deeds. *(Whispering.)* Find out, Klaus. Find out!

Klaus

(KLAUS is an apprentice to a Sorcerer. He/She is talking to an enchanted cat.)

KLAUS: Cat, you've got to help me. Before, I was just playing around with the Sorcerer's magic to make my work easier. But now, I've got to do something! Because the Sorcerer is evil! I heard him! He's planning a terrible spell. He wants to scramble the stars in the sky so that all their patterns will disappear! He's jealous of the stars! I always thought the Sorcerer was doing good magic, but I guess I was wrong. Tonight, I'm going to sneak into his workshop, and take his magic book. I know I can find a spell that will break his magic against the stars. But I need your help. Don't run away! Give me a chance! I know I haven't been the smartest apprentice, but I'm going to prove I can do something right. Are you going to help me or not?

CHAPTER FOUR
Scenes for Two Actors

The Gift

CHARACTERS: (2 w)
Jade, 13
Maddy, 10

SETTING:
Maddy's room

In this scene, JADE gives her once-favorite doll to her little sister, MADDY. This scene provides an excellent opportunity for exploring what can be communicated about characters and their emotions by how they handle props (the box, the dolls).

(MADDY is sitting on the floor of her room, playing the mom to her dolls.)

MADDY: No, you can't wear the red bow today. It's Lizzie's turn. *(Animating her dolls.)* "But she always gets to wear it first." "I do not!" "Yes, you do!" "Do not!" "Do so!" *(As Mom.)* Girls! Stop your fighting right this minute. Now let's see if we can find a solution! *(As doll.)* "I don't want to!" *(As Mom.)* Lizzie!

(JADE knocks on the door as she opens it. She is carrying a big box.)

JADE: Hey, how many people are in here? Sounds like the whole fifth grade.

MADDY: Lizzie and Angel are fighting again.

JADE: What's the problem?

MADDY: They're sisters.

JADE: Oh. That explains it.

MADDY: Lizzie wants to wear the red bow first, and Angel is mad.

JADE: I know how she feels! You took my purple sweater again, didn't you! I couldn't find it this morning —

MADDY: I just borrowed it.

JADE: On the day my friends and I always wear purple! Tina wears purple, I wear purple —

MADDY: Wednesdays used to be purple!

JADE: Now it's Tuesdays. Keep up!

MADDY: I can't keep up...with you.
  (MADDY crosses back to her dolls. There is an awkward silence between them.)

JADE: Look. Maddy. I didn't come in here to fight. I've been cleaning out my closet —

MADDY: You did *what*???

JADE: Don't faint! I do occasionally clean my room!

MADDY: How much did Mom pay you?

JADE: Nobody paid me. I needed to make room for my new stuff. So I put some old stuff in here. *(Handing her the box.)* Here.

MADDY: What's this?

JADE: Like I said. Old stuff.

MADDY. *(Quickly opening the box. She pulls out a doll.)* Jade! You put Jessica in a box? How's she gonna breathe?

JADE: She's a doll. She doesn't need to breathe! Ga, you are still such a baby!

MADDY: I'm not! But, she's your favorite! You made her a bed, and all those little drawers for her clothes, and —

JADE: All that stuff's in there, too.

MADDY: *(Looking through the box.)* Wow. Her pajamas and bathrobe! Where's her little dog on the leash?

JADE: It's in there. Somewhere. I guess. I mean, I haven't played with this stuff in years.

MADDY: She's beautiful! This is her school dress, right?

JADE: Yeah.

MADDY: Does she still have her little book bag?

JADE: Probably.

MADDY: *(Finding the book bag.)* Here it is. *(She begins to put it on the doll.)* Let's put this over your shoulder.

JADE: The other one. It goes on the other shoulder.

MADDY: Sorry.

JADE: And button her sweater.

MADDY: *(Giving Jessica a voice.)* "Oh gosh, I'm late for school —"

JADE: That's not how she talks.

MADDY: Then you make her talk.

(MADDY holds the doll out to JADE. But JADE does not take it.)

MADDY: Why won't you show me?

JADE: Just don't lose any of her stuff. Or cut her hair or anything.

MADDY: I can *keep* her?

JADE: And don't take her ribbons out either.

MADDY: You mean it?

JADE: You can keep her.

MADDY: Forever?

JADE: Yes.

(In the silence, MADDY understands what an important present this is. She carefully takes Jessica over to her other dolls.)

MADDY: Lizzie, Angel, this is Jessica. She was my sister's favorite doll. Now she's mine. Say hello, everybody. "Hi Jessica." "Hi." *(MADDY holds up Jessica to speak, but she doesn't dare use a voice.)* Jessica is being a little shy. She's not talking right now. So. What do you like to do Jessica? *(Pause.)* Any ideas?

JADE: She…likes tea parties.

MADDY: She does? What's your favorite color? Blue? Pink?

Come on, Jade, I've got two teapots. Which one will she like?

JADE: Your pink one. With the purple top.

MADDY: *(Getting her teapot.)* Tea time! Here's some for you. *(As Lizzie.)* "Thank you." And some for you. *(As Angel.)* "Oh, why thank you. It's delicious." *(Pouring tea for Jessica.)* And some for Jessica. *(MADDY looks at JADE.)*

JADE: *(Smiling, giving Jessica a voice.)* "Thank you."

MADDY: Is it good?

JADE: "It's wonderful."

MADDY: *(Imitating her sister's doll voice.)* "Wonderful." *(MADDY smiles at her big sister. Then she launches into play.)* Now, as soon as everyone's had enough, it will be time to start our lessons. Jessica has books in her book bag. Now I'm the teacher.

JADE: *(Leaving.)* See ya, Maddy.

MADDY: Bye Jade. Jessica will be just fine.

JADE: Promise?

MADDY: Yeah. Now, who wants to read first?

(JADE exits as MADDY sets up the dolls for a story.)

End of Scene.

Reel Stuff

Inspired in part by *Apollo: To the Moon*

CHARACTERS: (2 m)
    Eddie, 12
    Reuben, 12

SETTING:
    Eddie's room

> *EDDIE and REUBEN are best friends. They have been assigned to make a video for a class at school. They are at EDDIE's house, in his room, pitching ideas to each other. Both boys have very vivid imaginations, and like to use their voices, bodies, and available props.*

REUBEN: OK, Eddie. We can start our video like this. There's this spaceship, and it lands right beside the Washington Monument. *(He has a plastic model of a spaceship, and creates the landing moment, complete with great vocal sound effects.)* Then everybody runs around screaming! Then the army brings out hundreds of tanks and guns, but nothing happens. So they wait.

EDDIE: *(Accompanying his friend's description with scary music sounds.)* Be-du! Be-du!

REUBEN: And wait! More music, Eddie.

EDDIE: *(Picking up his cue.)* Be-du! Be-du!

REUBEN: Finally, the door of the spaceship slides back.*(He makes a spaceship-door-opening sound.)* And out walks this guy in a silver space suit.

EDDIE: Is he human?

REUBEN: He looks pretty human, so nobody gets too scared. But then, this big robot guy comes walking out.

EDDIE: I'll be the robot! I'll be the robot! *(EDDIE starts moving across the room with big slow monster steps.)*

REUBEN: He's made outta this special steel.

EDDIE: *(In big robot voice.)* Special steel.

REUBEN: And he's got no face.

(EDDIE pulls his shirt up over his face.)

REUBEN: OK. Now I'm the space guy. "I come in peace." But then this army guy shoots him in the arm. Ahh!!

EDDIE: *(Popping his head out of his shirt.)* Why do they shoot him?

REUBEN: That's what army guys do!

EDDIE: Oh.

REUBEN: Anyway!

(EDDIE resumes his robot stance and shirt-over-face.)

REUBEN: This makes the robot really mad, so he lifts up the visor on his face —

(EDDIE slowly pulls the shirt down.)

REUBEN: And he vaporizes the weapons of the army guys. *(Both boys make fabulous shooting and vaporizing noises.)* Then the space guy escapes. And he hides out where this kid named Bobby lives with his Mother. And Bobby and the space guy become friends. Then, the space guy says he wants to get all the scientists of the world together so he can tell them something really important. He says it will save the earth! Save the earth from something terrible. *(Bursting into scary music.)* Be-du! Be-du!

EDDIE: *(Joining in.)* Be-du, Be — Hey wait a minute. I've seen this movie. It's an old black-and-white flick!

REUBEN: Yeah, it's fantastic! *The Day the Earth Stood Still*.

EDDIE: But we're supposed to make our own movie for class.

REUBEN: So, we'll do a remake. I can play Bobby *and* the
    space guy —
EDDIE: *I'll* be the space guy.
REUBEN: You gotta be the robot.
EDDIE: But the robot doesn't talk.
REUBEN: That's why it's a remake, so you can talk.
EDDIE: I got another idea. What if we make a movie about
    two kids in a haunted house.
REUBEN: Boy, *that's* original!
EDDIE: Listen, this is cool. See, the house got built on top of
    an old graveyard. And at night, when the kids are trying
    to sleep, the ghosts of all the people buried under the
    house come tapping on the door — *(He taps creepily.)*
    And scratching on the windows — *(He scratches creep-
    ily.)* So the kids look out, and they see this figure — this
    guy who's got no bones who sucks out the eyeballs of
    children who won't go to sleep at night —
REUBEN: What are you talking about?
EDDIE: The flabby man. My aunt used to tell me about him
    to get me to go to sleep. Scary, huh, this guy who sucks
    out your eyeballs — *(EDDIE makes sucking sounds as
    the frightening flabby man.)*
REUBEN: That's not scary. That's gross!
EDDIE: We could use grapes for the eyeballs. They look like
    eyeballs when you take the skins off.
REUBEN: But how would we make a guy without any bones?
EDDIE: How are we gonna make a spaceship land in the mid-
    dle of Washington??!!
REUBEN: Scale models! Easy. I got 'em all right here. *(He
    heads for a box of stuff to pull out.)*
EDDIE: Wait! I got another idea. There's these two kids in a
    haunted house —
REUBEN: Again!
EDDIE: And their Mother locked them in there 'cause she's

crazy. And there's a pack of man-eating dogs who live in the basement and they tear away at the flesh of the boys. *(He imagines being chomped by one of the dogs.)* Ahhh!

REUBEN: What's the point?

EDDIE: And they manage to escape, but then they get kidnapped by these two crazy guys. They blindfold the kids, and tell them they're gonna drop them over a five-hundred-foot waterfall into a pool of piranhas if they don't tell them where the money is!

REUBEN: What'd they do with the money?

EDDIE: They hid it under the bricks in the fireplace of the haunted house, inside the bones of the guy that their crazy mother murdered when she went nuts after she saw a ghost in her mirror when she was a kid.

REUBEN: Jeez, Eddie!

EDDIE: What?

REUBEN: Why's everything gotta be so creepy with you? There's enough real stuff to be scared about. Why do you always make up more?

EDDIE: Your idea's scary, too.

REUBEN: But it's got a happy ending. All the people in the world come together, so they're not scared anymore.

EDDIE: Oh. I can do happy endings. So, how do you think a robot talks?

REUBEN: *(Walking and talking like the robot-monster.)* Like this. "I will save the earth!"

EDDIE: *(Joining in.)* "I will save the earth!"

REUBEN: "Come with me, in my spaceship. To worlds unknown."

EDDIE: I'll go get the camera.

(REUBEN takes out his plastic model of a spaceship and sails it upward as both boys make flying spaceship noises.)

End of Scene.

Above It All

CHARACTERS: (2 w)
Kali, 13
Jenna, 13

SETTING:
In a seat on a Ferris wheel

KALI and JENNA are best friends. KALI's parents are separated. Her Mom has brought KALI and JENNA to the beach. They are at an amusement park at the end of a boardwalk. A great challenge of the scene is to create the believability of a Ferris wheel ride with your voices, bodies, and reactions. As the scene begins, the girls have just been locked into a seat on the Ferris wheel.

KALI: Gotta breathe deep, Jenna. You'll be fine.
(JENNA tries to breathe deep.)
KALI: In. Out. In. Out. In — *(The Ferris wheel takes off.)* Up!
JENNA: *(Screaming.)* Ahh!
KALI: I can't believe you've never been on a Ferris wheel! Girl, you have been missin' it. *(They stop.)*
JENNA: Why'd we stop? Oh God, it's broken.
KALI: Relax! We gotta stop to let other people on. We do that all the way around.
JENNA: We're gonna stop? On the top?
KALI: That's the best.
JENNA: I can't believe I let you talk me into this! Are you sure we can't fall out?

KALI: What do you think this bar is for? Doin' flips? *(KALI gives their seat a little push, making it rock.)*

JENNA: Don't *do* that!

KALI: All Ferris-wheel pros swing the seat.

JENNA: I am not a pro! Let's get off, Kali.

KALI: We paid for this!

JENNA: I don't care. Whoa!*(They start again.)*

KALI: Wheee!

JENNA: Oh no! *(They stop almost at the top.)*

KALI: Check it out! You can see all the way down the beach. There's our hotel.

JENNA: *(Frozen in fear.)* Yeah.

KALI: And that's where my Mom got the umbrella, and the beach chairs. Man, that sales guy was good-lookin'!

JENNA: Yeah.

KALI: Jenna, what's the point?

JENNA: Point?

KALI: Of dyin' fifty feet up in the air because you forgot to breathe.

JENNA: Right. *(The Ferris wheel turns again.)* Ahh!
(This time it stops past the top, in that place where you feel like you are dangling above everything.)

KALI: Right here, right here, yes! I love this stop. Right past the top. Feel it? It's like you're sailing above everything. Can't see any other seats — nobody! Are your eyes open?

JENNA: Barely.

KALI: Jenna. Come on. Take a chance.
(JENNA opens her eyes slowly.)

KALI: See the lights? All the way down the boardwalk! Like a mirror of what you see when you look up. Stars! Everywhere.

JENNA: I like stars.

KALI: Then look up! Forget about down.

JENNA: OK. Wow. It *is* pretty. *(The Ferris wheel starts to go down.)*

KALI: Wooo-hooo! Goin' down. And around! See. Once it gets goin', it's great.

JENNA: I keep leaving my stomach somewhere.

KALI: Stars! Look up! Always look up!

JENNA: Right! Wow. I like this part. It's just when we get all the way to the top, and over — *(That's where they are.)* I feel like I'm falling off the world.

KALI: That's how I feel on the ground, not up here.

JENNA: Huh?

KALI: Forget it.

JENNA: Forget what?

KALI: This is where I like to be, spinnin' so fast, everything is lights and colors. Everything's big. Don't have to notice the details.

JENNA: What details?

(The Ferris wheel turns to another stopped position, but KALI is quiet for the first time.)

JENNA: Kali! What did you mean?

KALI: What do you think I meant?

JENNA: Is it your Dad? Did he call you?

KALI: Dad? Dad who! I wish this thing would start turning again!

JENNA: He's not supposed to call you. The lawyers told him not to.

KALI: Yeah, well, lawyers think they got all the power, but they don't.

JENNA: Does your Mom know?

KALI: Why should I tell her? She can't be any madder at him than she is now.

JENNA: You've gotta tell somebody! He's not supposed to call you! *(Ferris wheel starts to move again.)*

KALI: Thank you, Ferris wheel. Don't be over!

JENNA: Kali!

KALI: Keep turning! Spinning —

JENNA: We're going to stop, Kali.

KALI: We're stayin' above everything. Forever!

    (The Ferris wheel stops.)

JENNA: You've got to tell your Mom. Last time —

KALI: Last time I believed him. Last time he told me he'd come back for good. If he thinks I'll ever believe him again... *(Calling down.)* Turn! Keep turning! *(The Ferris wheel turns.)*

JENNA: This is the last stop. Then we get off.

    (Pause as KALI looks down sadly at the ground.)

JENNA: Don't look down yet, Kali. Look at the big things.

KALI: Stars and lights.

JENNA: And the whole big ocean.

KALI: Why does it have to be over?

JENNA: I can help, Kali. Let's go talk to your Mom.

KALI: I —

JENNA: You have to.

KALI: Goin' down.

    (The girls reach their final stop.)

End of Scene.

Family Tug-O-Wars

CHARACTERS: (1 m, 1 w)
Zach, 11
Sonya, 12

SETTING:
Sonya's Room

SONYA and ZACH are cousins. There is a family party going on at SONYA's house. SONYA's Mom has just embarrassed her by revealing something she read in SONYA's diary. As the scene opens, SONYA pulls a suitcase out from under her bed and begins to stuff clothes angrily into it.

ZACH: *(Offstage.)* Sonya! Sonya!

SONYA: Leave me alone!!

ZACH: *(Entering.)* What are you doing?

SONYA: What does it look like?

ZACH: Grandma's all mad because you stomped out of her birthday party —

SONYA: Because of my Mom!

ZACH: She was kidding you! Come on, you gotta come back downstairs. We're lighting the candles on the cake.

SONYA: No way! I'm never going back down there. If my Mom thinks she can read my diary, and then blab my most personal thoughts in front of every relative I have, then she doesn't deserve to be a Mom. I'm leaving.

ZACH: Don't be crazy. Where would you go?

SONYA: To Kim's house. Her parents are perfect. They would never read her diary. I'll go live with them.

ZACH: Have you asked Kim about that?

SONYA: She's my best friend. She'll understand. Where are my sweaters? It'll be cold soon.

ZACH: You're not really going to run away.

SONYA: Watch me! I can't take it! She snoops through my drawers. I came in here yesterday, and she was digging around in my closet.

ZACH: Maybe she was trying to straighten it up.

SONYA: But it's my stuff!

ZACH: And it's her house.

SONYA: But in my room it's private!

ZACH: You're not doing anything bad — drugs or something?

SONYA: Now *you're* crazy. I'm not that stupid. I just want some privacy.

ZACH: So ask her for some.

SONYA: I can't talk to her. She doesn't listen to me. I'll start to tell her something about how I feel, then she says, "You don't think that, do you?" So what I am supposed to say? If she criticizes what I say the minute I say it, why should I say anything?

ZACH: Wow.

SONYA: *And* she's a blackmailer! "If you don't finish your science project, you won't be going to the movies with Kim on Friday." I'm old enough to make my own choices about how I spend my time!

ZACH: Not if you haven't finished your science project.

SONYA: What kind of a cousin are you? Here I am in the biggest crisis of my life, and this is how you help me? You're just like my Mom. Maybe you should be her kid instead of me.

ZACH: Want me to help you pack?

SONYA: What?

ZACH: You're right. It sounds really bad between you guys. Running away might really make a point.

SONYA: Exactly. You are absolutely right. You know how I'm gonna get out?

ZACH: How?

SONYA: Sheets.

ZACH: Sheets?

SONYA: *(Struggling to tie sheets together.)* I'm going to tie my sheets together, like this, then tie one end to this chair by the window. Then I can use the sheets like a rope to climb out of the window and down into the street.

ZACH: Why don't you just wait 'till everybody's gone, then go down the stairs?

SONYA: That's too easy! This is how you're supposed to do it. It's more dramatic.

ZACH: *(Looking out the window.)* I see. Yeah. That'll be cool. Come on, I'll help you.

SONYA: I...I haven't finished packing.

ZACH: Looks like you have to me. *(He crosses to SONYA's suitcase and closes it.)* Aren't you gonna go?

SONYA: Yes! This is the last moment I will ever spend in this house.

ZACH: *(Handing her one end of the sheet.)* OK. Get a good grip. I'll tie this end to the chair.

SONYA: *(Pulling on the sheet.)* Wait a minute.

ZACH: *(Pulling on his end.)* Don't pull, Sonya. I'm trying to tie it.

(The sheet pulling turns into a tug-of-war.)

SONYA: I'll tie it. It's my escape!

ZACH: I'm just helping! Let go.

SONYA: It's my sheet. Let go!

ZACH: No!

SONYA: Yes!

ZACH: *(Playfully.)* Tug-of-war!

SONYA: Let go!

ZACH: OK.

(ZACH lets go. SONYA flies backwards, and lands on her bottom. The cousins look at one another, then start to laugh.)

ZACH: Got ya. I always beat you in tug-of-wars.

SONYA: Yeah, well I win the sack races!

ZACH: *And* the greasy watermelon races! *(They laugh.)*

SONYA: Why do we always play stupid games at family parties? *(SONYA looks at her suitcase, opens it, and dumps all the clothes out onto her bed.)*

ZACH: Grandma's cake is probably on fire by now.

SONYA: Probably.

ZACH: You know, I could get you a box with a lock.

SONYA: What?

ZACH: For your diary.

SONYA: Thanks, Zach.

ZACH: And I'll coach you, too. I know how to talk to Moms.

SONYA: Glad somebody does.

ZACH: *(Jumping up.)* Come on. We gotta sing "Happy Birthday."

SONYA: I'm comin'. *(The cousins exit.)*

End of Scene.

Boy Talk

Adapted from *What Part Will I Play?*

CHARACTERS: (2 w)
>   Chase, 14
>   Desiree, 13

SETTING:
>   An empty stage in a theatre

>   *CHASE and DESIREE are at an audition for a play. The director of the play is delayed, so the thirteen girls who have come to audition have been forced to interact. CHASE is a tomboy, dressed in jeans, a boy's shirt, and baseball cap. DESIREE, who is very attractive and mature, is wearing a tight leotard and a short skirt. As the scene begins, CHASE tentatively approaches DESIREE — her opposite "type."*

CHASE: Desiree?

DESIREE: Yeah?

CHASE: Can I ask you a few things?

DESIREE: Sure. What about?

CHASE: Well, you seem…I mean you look…I mean you dress like…you know how to…you know.

DESIREE: What are you talking about?

CHASE: Boys.

DESIREE: What do you want to know?

CHASE: Everything.

DESIREE: In five minutes or less?

CHASE: Sure.

DESIREE: Come on, Chase. What do you want to know?

CHASE: Well, how do you…get them to want to be with you?

DESIREE: How do you think?

CHASE: Yeah. But I don't have…what you have, so I think I'd better try a different tactic.

DESIREE: Well, for starters, you could stop pretending you're a guy.

CHASE: I'm not pretending I'm a guy.

DESIREE: Then why do you dress, talk, and act like one?

CHASE: Because I like to.

DESIREE: So choose. Either be one or be with one.

CHASE: But what do you do when you're with one?

DESIREE: Come back when you're older.

CHASE: I'm older than you, Desiree. Come on!

DESIREE: Well, you talk…sometimes for hours on the phone.

CHASE: What about?

DESIREE: Anything.

CHASE: Do they talk back?

DESIREE: Most of the time.

CHASE: I wouldn't know what to say. I've always been friends — you know, pals with guys.

DESIREE: Haven't you ever had a friend you can tell anything to? Who you can laugh with and feel silly with?

CHASE: A couple.

DESIREE: That's all a boyfriend is, plus a little more.

CHASE: It's the little more that's got me worried.

DESIREE: When the right time comes, you'll know it.

CHASE: I hope I don't miss it.

DESIREE: You won't.

CHASE: You think?

DESIREE: Sure.

CHASE: Thanks, Desiree. I knew you'd have the answers.

(She crosses away from DESIREE.)

DESIREE: *(To herself, revealing a far less confident self.)*
Yeah. Desiree knows it all. If she only knew.
(DESIREE sits alone.)

End of Scene.

First Impressions

Adapted from *What Part Will I Play?*

CHARACTERS: (2 w)
Marley, 13
Jessie, 12

SETTING:
An empty stage in a theater

MARLEY and JESSIE are at an audition for a play. The director of the play is delayed, so the thirteen girls who have come to audition have been forced to interact. But they know one another by outward image only. MARLEY gives the impression of being very tough — a "stoner." JESSIE is curious, a "wanna-be" popular girl. In this scene, JESSIE is speaking to MARLEY for the first time.

JESSIE: Marley?
MARLEY: What do you want.
JESSIE: Nothing.
MARLEY: Good.
   (Neither girl says anything for a moment.)
JESSIE: What's it like?
MARLEY: What?
JESSIE: Doing drugs.
MARLEY: Who says I do drugs?
JESSIE: You've got to do drugs. You're a stoner.
MARLEY: Well, sure. Some.
JESSIE: And knives and stuff. Don't you guys play with knives and stuff at your parties?
MARLEY: Where do you get your information?
JESSIE: School. And you play heavy metal music while painting graffiti on your parents' garages, right?

MARLEY: Look, I'm not a criminal.

JESSIE: Hey, that's just what I've heard about you guys.

MARLEY: You have no idea what I'm about.

JESSIE: So, tell me.

MARLEY: Why should I?

JESSIE: Because if you don't do drugs or slash up couches, I might like you. I like your clothes.

MARLEY: *(Laughing, liking her.)* Aren't you afraid of ruining your image?

JESSIE: What image? Half the time I'm not anybody. *Most* of the time. I'm just Jeff's shadow. He's my boyfriend. I've got to break up with him. *(Pause.)* Man, why am I telling you this?

MARLEY: Cause you like my clothes?

(The girls smile at one another. An uneasy friendship is beginning.)

MARLEY: So what's going on?

JESSIE: Well, Jeff, he's... Are you sure you want to talk to me?

MARLEY: I'm listening, aren't I?

JESSIE: We fight a lot. It's stupid. We don't even like to be together anymore.

MARLEY: So tell him to get lost.

JESSIE: But all my friends are his friends. I'd be alone if we broke up.

MARLEY: It's no good being alone.

JESSIE: So, tell me about you.

MARLEY: Well, stoners are —

JESSIE: No. I want to know about you.

MARLEY: I'm telling you!

JESSIE: So, you're just a stoner?

MARLEY: No.

JESSIE: Good. So let's talk.

(The girls move closer to one another.)

End of Scene.

Talkin' Trash

Adapted from *Broken Rainbows*

CHARACTERS: (2 m)
Joel, 14
Damond, 14

SETTING:
A curbside and the back of a recycling truck

JOEL and DAMOND are both volunteers in a youth program that helps with city recycling. JOEL, who is white and Jewish, has just moved into the neighborhood with his recently divorced mother. DAMOND is African-American. As the scene begins, they enter with large recycling crates. They are picking up and dumping cans, bottles, and newspapers into their crates, then carrying them into the large bins on the recycling truck. These actions can all be mimed.

DAMOND: Man, this must be a six-pack-a-day neighborhood. What're they doin' with all these nasty cans?

JOEL: People don't think about it. Buy a Coke, drink it, throw the can away, like that's the end of it.

DAMOND: "The end" is me busting my butt.

JOEL: "The end" is environmental catastrophe!

DAMOND: Whatever you say, Professor Greenpeace. *(Muttering.)* Why d'they have to paint these trucks all circus-lookin'? Bright colors and kiddie names: "Paper tiger" for white paper, "Mr. News" for newspaper —

JOEL: The trucks are supposed to attract attention, so people will think about recycling.

(*Sound of the horn of a car driving past. DAMOND ducks behind one of the bins, pushing JOEL out of the way.*)

DAMOND: Outta my way, man.

JOEL: What're you doin'?

DAMOND: Dag!

JOEL: What's the deal?

DAMOND: That was Lamont!

JOEL: Huh?

DAMOND: Lamont, man!

JOEL: Oh. Don't want your friends seein' ya doin' this?

DAMOND: You got that straight.

JOEL: Why'd you volunteer for this program, if you don't care about the environment?

DAMOND: I'm just puttin' in my time on the bottom, so I can step up to the top.

JOEL: Huh?

DAMOND: I got bigger plans than you could ever dream of.

(*The boys look at one another, continuing to size each other up.*)

JOEL: Listen, I don't know too many people around here, so I'll stay on the front line.

DAMOND: Yeah?

JOEL: Feel free to hide behind me when your friends drive by.

DAMOND: (*Laughing.*) You're all right, Joel. So, you're the new kid in town?

JOEL: Very observant.

DAMOND: And you haven't had my tour of the neighborhood?

JOEL: What tour?

DAMOND: Step right up, my man, for Damond's Grayline

cruise of our fair community. Come on, the truck's pullin' out.

(They jump on the truck. They mime the truck pulling out and moving down the street. The truck's radio is on, playing rock or rap music.)

DAMOND: On your left we have three to five small streets, with thirty to fifty identical houses, filled with three to five hundred identical people.

JOEL: What're you talking about?

DAMOND: Asians, man. Every one of 'em. From China, Vietnam, I don't know where else. Millions of 'em. Count 'em!

JOEL: Right

DAMOND: Down that road you will find enchilada land.

JOEL: Hispanics live over there?

DAMOND: "His"panics, "her"spanics—

JOEL: Very funny.

DAMOND: Then further over, way over, locked away on your right, we find the land of milk and honey. God's chosen—

JOEL: Yeah, OK.

DAMOND: The Goldbergs, the Silverbergs, the Moneybergs—

JOEL: I'm Jewish, OK? Lay off.

(The truck comes to a stop. MUSIC fades as the boys get off to do another collection.)

DAMOND: Sorry, man.

JOEL: Half-Jewish. Maybe three-quarters.

DAMOND: You don't know?

JOEL: My Dad was — *is* — Jewish, and my Mom is Italian-Jewish, but she —

DAMOND: All Italians are Catholics, man.

JOEL: Not all... Forget it. It's not worth it.

DAMOND: Whatever you say.

(They work in silence for a moment.)

DAMOND: I'll chill on the Jewish jokes. Catholic, too.

JOEL: You're too kind. It won't matter what jokes you tell next week.

DAMOND: Why's that?

JOEL: Fact is, Damond, we may not be partners much longer. You may be slingin' "peli-cans" all by your lonesome while I'm…doin' something else.

DAMOND: Are you applying for that management internship?

JOEL: Stay tuned.

DAMOND: Don't mess with me. Are you? Cause I'm gonna get it.

JOEL: That's a joke. *(The sound of the truck horn. JOEL grabs his crate and begins to exit to truck.)* Hustle, man. *(Looking back.)* Come on, hustle.
(JOEL bustles off, but DAMOND takes his time with his bin.)

DAMOND: *(To himself.)* No, man. *You* stay tuned. *(DAMOND exits.)*

End of Scene.

Facing the Waves

Adapted from *Surf's Up*

CHARACTERS: (1 m, 1 w)
Kitt (m), 12–13
Shine (w), 12–13

SETTING:
The beach

KITT and SHINE, both 12-13, have been friends since they were young kids. They meet every summer when they visit their grandparents in Florida. It is the very beginning of the summer surfing season. KITT is an excellent surfer; SHINE is an aspiring one. As the scene begins, SHINE is meeting KITT for a day on the beach.

KITT: Where you been, beginner? Aren't you stoked?

SHINE: That's "excited" in surfer-speak, right?

KITT: All right, Shine! You're learnin' the lingo! The new vibe is clear. Paddle out and charge or be labeled a small wave guy. You, however, are still a grommet on the long board.

SHINE: I'm workin' on it. I just need more practice.

KITT: It's all in the stance. Left foot down the board. Right foot across it. *(SHINE and KITT both practice the surfing moves.)* Means you face the waves when you ride to the right. Gotta look into the face of Mother Ocean.

SHINE and KITT: *(Sharing a surfer handshake / motto.)* Be cat-chin' some ac-tion!

SHINE: So you gonna help tomorrow?

KITT: With what?

SHINE: The beach clean up. We need everybody.

KITT: You still beating the eco-warrior drum?

SHINE: Somebody's got to. The trash has gotten really bad.

KITT: Shine. There are only so many hours in a day. And only so many waves in an hour. I can't spend those precious hours changing the world. That's your job.

SHINE: We can start early. Pick up what the tide's left behind —

KITT: I got other plans for then, and for now. We are talkin' some excellent waves out there! Let's go!

SHINE: Kitt, wait. I don't think we should go in.

KITT: You scared of the big ride? Those monster waves are thanks to Mother Nature. A week of storms means we make a killer score! You comin'?

SHINE: It's not the waves.

KITT: Then what's the deal?

SHINE: Have you seen the drainpipe? The one up the beach?

KITT: Oh no. Here comes another eco-alert.

SHINE: There's more than river water in there. Go smell it. It's nasty.

KITT: It's always nasty.

SHINE: But it's never been this bad.

KITT: Then maybe you and your tribe should make some more signs. "No dumping. We live downstream." That was my favorite of all your plans to help the environment. Spray-painting signs — who cares if your spray cans deplete the ozone —

SHINE: We switched to paint brushes!

KITT: Or even better, when you had your Dad drive you all over town, burning up gas and oil to pick up people's stuff to recycle.

SHINE: At least I'm trying to help!

KITT: Yeah, but you don't get it. Shine, there are some things you just can't change. Take the drainpipe —

SHINE: Yeah?

KITT: It's all part of the bigger journey. People are gonna drive, so their cars are gonna drip oil. Once an oil glob goes plop into a parking lot, boom, it is on its way. *(He becomes the oil glob, surfing.)* Washed by the rain, into the storm drains, zippin' through the underground city of pipes, then pow — into the ocean. Next thing you know, I'm wiping that oil glob off my board. It's a drag, but you gotta dodge the dredge if you wanna ride the waves. *(He starts to exit.)*

SHINE: I don't think it's oil this time. It's something else.

KITT: You comin' or not?

SHINE: Give it till tomorrow, Kitt. Maybe whatever it is will get washed out farther. Outta the surf zone.

KITT: Shine. A real surfer cannot be afraid of the unknown. I'm out there. *(He crosses toward the beach.)*

SHINE: *(Calling after him.)* Then don't stay in too long! And keep your mouth closed! *(To herself.)* Please. *(SHINE watches as KITT exits.)*

End of Scene.

Impact Zone Adapted from *Surf's Up*

CHARACTERS: (1 m, 1 w)
   Kitt (m), 12–13
   Shine (w), 12–13

SETTING:
   The beach

   Best friends, KITT and SHINE, both 12-13, have been at the beach for two weeks, visiting their grandparents. In an earlier scene (see p.84), SHINE was worried about what she believed to be pollution going into the ocean from a city drainpipe. KITT ignored her warnings, and continued to go into the ocean. But now the smell from the drainpipe has improved, no warnings have been posted, so SHINE's fear has passed. As this scene begins, SHINE is on the beach, practicing her surfing stance.

SHINE: I am ready to hit the waves.
   (KITT enters. He is not his usual self.)
SHINE: Finally! Where you been, Kitt? You promised to give me a long board lesson. Didn't your Mother teach you to keep your promises?
KITT: Sorry.
SHINE: At least all that drainpipe dreck is gone. You know, you may be right, Kitt. Maybe I sound the eco-alarm before I should. Anyway, I am ready to ride. So, I hug the curl, right? And stay close to the white water but don't let it snag me. *(No response.)* Right?
KITT: Yeah.

SHINE: And so I don't get creamed by a dumper, keep my tail outta the impact zone. *(SHINE imitates a wave breaking on top of her.)*

KITT: That won't be easy.

SHINE: I can handle it. I'm stoked!

KITT: You don't get it, do you. It's all one big impact zone now. Impacting big time.

SHINE: What are you talking about?

KITT: My uncle. He knows a guy who works downtown for the place that takes what we flush and turns it into *acceptable* mush —

SHINE: Yeah, OK. The sewage treatment plant. I don't need details.

KITT: Yeah, well our grandparents' beachside burg is gettin' too big. The underground city of pipes can't handle it.

SHINE: Handle what?

KITT: All the flushes *and* the extra rushes of water from all the rain. Sometimes some of what's flowin' hangs a sharp right, and gets dumped in the river, before it makes it to the sewage treatment plant. If that happened, then raw crap from the river's been flowin' right into —

SHINE: Our drainpipe!

KITT: I've been surfing in toxic soup! In raw sewage that got "diverted" right into my home — my ocean.

SHINE: It couldn't have been very much. Somebody would have done something.

KITT: What if it was, and nobody did anything? Or nobody knew?

SHINE: Then don't go in. Nobody should go in!

KITT: You gonna ask me not to breathe, too? *(SHINE is silent.)* This feels like when we were kids. Remember? We'd build a big sand wall in front of our castle tryin' to keep the waves from wipin' it out. We never could stop 'em. We'll never stop this, either.

SHINE: Don't say that. Maybe it's all gone now, anyway.

KITT: Maybe it's not. *(Pause.)* Listen, I didn't meet you yesterday, or the day before —

SHINE: Yeah, why didn't you?

KITT: Cause I've been feelin'…I don't know…strange. Maybe I'm paranoid, but my eyes have been burning, my throat.

SHINE: Kitt!!

KITT: I don't know.

SHINE: You should get checked out.

KITT: And have some doctor tell me "You've got a respiratory infection" or "You've got hepatitis A or B or Z" cause you've been paddlin' out into what you thought was the most beautiful, the most sacred of all places!

SHINE: It is. The ocean still is.

KITT: But it's messed up. People are messing it up! Why? Why during my life, my time with her, you know? *(SHINE does not have an answer.)*

KITT: How are you gonna fix it?

SHINE: Me?!

KITT: You've got to. Somebody's got to. I don't know where to start.

SHINE: What can I do?

KITT: Please, Shine.

SHINE: OK. I'll try — try to find out what's really going on. And then we'll fix it. Somehow. Promise.

KITT: You think it's too late?

SHINE: It can't be. Come on.

(KITT and SHINE exit together.)

End of Scene.

Stand Off Adapted from *Blessings*

CHARACTERS: (2 w)
  Katie, 13–14
  Rene, 13–14

SETTING:
The living room of a mountain cabin

KATIE and RENE are the daughters of high-school friends who are having a reunion in a cabin in the mountains of California. KATIE's father brought her along as a surprise for RENE. What the adults don't know (or remember) is that RENE and KATIE did not get along at all at the last reunion. KATIE is a super-achiever, first in her class for everything. RENE is a very talented water-colorist, but she struggles with severe learning disabilities. During the play, the girls learn that they have much more in common than they ever dreamed.

In this scene, KATIE has just performed one of her orig-inal songs for the group. Now the girls are left alone together for the first time.

KATIE: *(Calling down the hall.)* Good night, Dad. See you in the morning bright.
  (KATIE and RENE look at one another. RENE moves to get her sleeping bag, and starts to unroll it on the floor. KATIE pauses uncomfortably.)
KATIE: You can sleep on the couch. I know you weren't expecting to have to share this room.

RENE: I'd rather sleep on the floor. It's better for your back.

KATIE: What?

RENE: I learned that in movement class.

KATIE: You take dance?

RENE: Movement. It's different.

KATIE: I had to take a dance class last year. It was awful. But I had the lead in the school musical and I had to dance, so they made me take it. And then in the show, I sang really terribly.

RENE: Why do you say things like that?

KATIE: Like what?

RENE: You just sang great for everybody. And didn't you write the song, too?

KATIE: I'm not as good as I should be.

RENE: And you've got to be the best?

(KATIE turns away from RENE. Silence, but then KATIE begins to laugh.)

RENE: What? Why are you laughing?

KATIE: That was so funny when you opened the popcorn while it was still popping! It was like a white volcano exploding! *(KATIE mimes popcorn exploding from a popper and flying everywhere.)* Didn't you hear everybody telling you not to?

RENE: No.

KATIE: Your Mom was talking right to you.

RENE: Sometimes I just…can't listen. It's the way I am.

KATIE: Oh. I didn't know you had a hearing problem…on top of everything else.

RENE: I don't have — Forget it. *(RENE crosses to her sleeping bag.)*

KATIE: I know you don't want me here. You might as well say it. *(RENE is still silent.)*

KATIE: You can ignore me. It's OK. I can't believe I missed a whole day of school just driving here. I'll probably fail because I missed class today.

RENE: Yeah, it's real tough on you straight-A students, isn't it.

(Now it's KATIE's turn to be silent. She merely looks at RENE.)

RENE: Sorry if I'm not real sympathetic.

(RENE gets up and crosses to the lamp to turn it off.)

KATIE: *(Turning over to go to sleep.)* I'll probably fail.

(RENE turns off the light. She is left in the glow of the moonlight.)

End of Scene.

The Looking Spot *Adapted from Blessings*

CHARACTERS: (2 w)
> Katie, 13–14
> Rene, 13–14

SETTING:
> The "looking spot"

In this scene from Blessings (see an earlier scene from the play on page 90), KATIE has just performed a song that she says she has written — both the words and the music. But KATIE's father's girlfriend recognizes the words to be a poem by Rossetti. KATIE's father confronts her about her dishonesty, and KATIE runs from the cabin, crying. RENE is challenged by the adults to go after KATIE. In this scene, RENE has found KATIE and is taking her to the looking spot, an outcropping of rocks high above the valley below.

(RENE is climbing up on to the rock. KATIE is lagging behind.)

RENE: See? We made it. Now you've got to look.

(KATIE remains at a distance. She is silent.)

RENE: Look out. Pick something. *(RENE sits.)*

KATIE: Why?

RENE: See that tree? It's not the same as the others. Or the stream. See it?

KATIE: I was just caught lying in front of all those people and you want me to look at the trees?

RENE: It'll help.

KATIE: I don't want your help.

RENE: Then why'd you come with me?

(KATIE looks at RENE. Finally KATIE sits down on the rocks.)

RENE: Over there, there's a town. The roads look like strings. See them? *(No reply.)* Katie, tell me what's wrong.

KATIE: You were there! You saw.

RENE: Why'd you do it? Why would you steal somebody's poem?

KATIE: I had to.

RENE: Can't you write your own words?

KATIE: What are they? I don't have any words of my own. Now my Dad knows I'm a liar. Knows I'm a fake.

RENE: So talk to him.

KATIE: No.

RENE: He's your Dad.

KATIE: So? You can't understand...what it's like. I don't know how to be anything...but everybody has to think I'm...the best...and now no one...

RENE: Katie. Stop shaking. Please. What can you see?

KATIE: Nothing. Falling. Floating. I... *(KATIE takes a step towards the edge of the rocks.)*

RENE: Katie, what are — stop it!

KATIE: I hate her!

RENE: What? Who?

KATIE: Katie! Me! I hate myself if I win and I hate myself if I don't. It's a contest. Always. With myself.

RENE: I'm in a contest with *life* every day. I can't read a clock. I get lost in my own house! There's always something me...to *trip* me...something I can't do! But I just *do*.

KATIE: I can't do that. I don't know how.

RENE: *(Pause.)* You've never failed? At anything? Ever?

KATIE: *(Shaking her head.)* It's terrible…to always be the best.

RENE: I wish I had your problem.

KATIE: I wish I had yours.

(They are silent in a moment of recognition of one another.)

RENE: Katie, are you scared of school?

KATIE: Yeah.

RENE: Just like me?

KATIE: Just like you.

(KATIE and RENE sit quietly. RENE looks out across the mountains.)

RENE: Look. It's the light from the lighthouse. See it? You don't see that very often. What do you see?

KATIE: *(Looking out for the first time.)* Clouds.

RENE: What else?

KATIE: Colors.

RENE: Where?

KATIE: There. There's yellow — on a rock. I've never seen that before.

(The girls smile and look out across the mountains.)

End of Scene.

Wasn't He Wearing a Waistcoat?
Adapted from *Alice*

CHARACTERS: (2 w)
Alice, 11
Lorina, 12

SETTING:
A river bank on a golden summer afternoon in England in 1862

ALICE and LORINA are sisters. Their governess, Miss Lewisham, has told them they can have a tea party by the river before continuing their lessons. In my adaptation of this classic story, ALICE is a playful, mischievous know-it-all, while LORINA is shy and insecure.

(ALICE races on, giggling, clutching her sister LORINA's book.)

LORINA: *(Offstage.)* Alice! *(Entering.)* Alice! Honestly! *(LORINA holds Dinah, the cat, in her arms and has a picnic basket.)* It is *my* book!

ALICE: But I have to practice. *(ALICE balances the book on her bonneted head and begins to walk in a stately fashion.)* Walking. Like a queen.

LORINA: *(Putting down basket.)* You ought to practice your lessons.

ALICE: *Bow* when you speak before her majesty.

LORINA: *(Setting out the cloth and teacups.)* Miss Lewisham will be ever so cross.

ALICE: She won't. I'm the brightest girl she ever taught. She told me so herself. Didn't she, Dinah, darling.

(ALICE tosses the book down, and plays with Dinah. LORINA cradles her book.)

ALICE: The brightest girl in the world. Lorina! Put your bonnet on this instant.

LORINA: Ladies never wear their bonnets during tea.

ALICE: But ladies always wear their bonnets out-of-doors. Mother said.

(LORINA puts her bonnet on.)

LORINA: But it's so hot.

ALICE: Use your fan.

LORINA: Young ladies never carry fans. Oh, I *think* it's "never" —

ALICE: Then we shall be grown-up ladies. *(Prompting her sister.)* "How do you do, your Highness."

LORINA: *(Picking up the game.)* "How do you—

ALICE: Lorina! Hold your teacup *thusly!*

LORINA: Honestly, Alice, you are worse than Miss Lewisham. I shall decide how we spend our tea. I *am* the oldest.

ALICE: But I shall be the biggest. One day, I'm sure I shall.

(A momentary standoff between the sisters. But LORINA knows that, somehow, ALICE is right. LORINA retreats into her book.)

ALICE: Lorina, one mustn't read during teatime!

LORINA: But there's a rather nice poem…

ALICE: Can you recite it all by heart?

LORINA: Not yet.

ALICE: I know six poems, all perfectly.

LORINA: Don't you want to hear this one?

ALICE: *(Standing, preparing to recite.)* To recite, fold one's hands thusly, chin up, feet together.

LORINA: *(Ignoring her.)* This is such a lovely poem, Alice. Rather dreamy.

ALICE: *(Reciting, complete with hand gestures.)* "How doth the little busy bee improve each shining hour. And gather honey all the day from every opening flower." *(Buzzing around.)* It's good to be a busy bee. *(Jumping down to play with Dinah.)* Isn't it, darling kitty? *(Pretending that Dinah is speaking.)* "It is indeed your majesty."

LORINA: I can't imagine being a bee.

ALICE: That doesn't surprise me in the least. You never imagine anything.

(LORINA buries herself in her book.)

ALICE: I know much more of the poem. *(ALICE thumps the cat down again as she jumps up to continue to recite.)*

LORINA: Alice. *(Picking up Dinah.)* You must be gentle. You'll hurt her feelings.

ALICE: "How skillfully she builds her cell. How neat she spreads the wax…" *(She stops, as if she has seen something.)* What was that?

LORINA: There, there, Dinah. What was what?

ALICE: *(Looking about curiously.)* I just saw…and I'm quite sure…he wore a waistcoat and gloves.

LORINA: The bee?

ALICE: The rabbit. The white rabbit. Didn't you see him?

LORINA: A rabbit? In a waistcoat.

ALICE: *(As if seeing him again.)* And a pocket watch. I thought he had a pocket watch!

LORINA: You're being quite silly, Alice. Isn't she, Dinah.

(LORINA continues to stroke the cat while ALICE moves closer and closer to the rabbit hole.)

ALICE: A rabbit doesn't need to know the time. Why ever should he need a watch. Mr. Rabbit?

LORINA: Quite silly, indeed.

ALICE: White rabbit! *(She disappears into the rabbit hole.)*
LORINA: That's enough, Alice. *(Looks up.)* Alice? Alice. If you're playing another of your tricks on me, I shall tell Miss Lewisham. *(Discovering that ALICE has truly vanished.)* Alice? Alice!! *(LORINA picks up Dinah and races off.)*

End of Scene.

CHAPTER FIVE
Scenes for Four Actors

Hide and Seek

CHARACTERS: (2 m, 2 w)
Natalie, 12–13
Mina, 12–13
Clayton, 12–13
James, 12–13

SETTING:
A bathhouse next to a swimming pool

NATALIE, MINA, CLAYTON, and JAMES are friends. They are at a swimming pool party. There is a bathhouse next to the pool. The bathhouse has a place for hanging up your clothes and putting your bags, and two changing rooms. It is near the end of the party. As the scene begins, NATALIE and MINA have just run into the bathhouse, attempting to hide from CLAYTON and JAMES.

MINA: In here!
NATALIE: Are you crazy? This is the first place they'll look!
CLAYTON: *(Offstage.)* Where'd they go?
NATALIE: Quick!
    (NATALIE and MINA both throw beach towels over themselves to hide. CLAYTON and JAMES enter.)
CLAYTON: You said they were going back into the pool!
JAMES: That's what Natalie said.
CLAYTON: *(Calling for them.)* Hey Mina! Natalie! Maybe they're in the basement. *(CLAYTON starts to leave.)*

JAMES: Wait up! *(Quietly to CLAYTON.)* Don't you get it? They're hiding.

CLAYTON: Hiding?

JAMES: *(Pointing to the bathhouse.)* In there!

CLAYTON: Huh?

JAMES: In the bathhouse!

CLAYTON: Oh!

JAMES: *(In a big voice.)* Yeah, you're *right*, Clayton. Bet they're in the basement. Let's just go on back into the party. *(The boys are sneaking into the bathhouse. They spy the girls huddled under the beach towels.)*

CLAYTON: Yeah. Who wants to swim anymore anyway.

JAMES: Yeah, who wants to.

CLAYTON: Guess we'll just have to — *(Ripping the towels off.)* expose you!

NATALIE: Clayton!

JAMES: Great hiding place!

NATALIE: *(To MINA.)* Yeah, great.

MINA: Well! They didn't find us right away!

CLAYTON: What'd you run away for anyway?

NATALIE: You were following us. Why were you following us?

MINA: Yeah, why?

JAMES: Try listening and he might tell you.

NATALIE: I can't imagine caring about anything you have to say.

CLAYTON: Really?

NATALIE: Really.

CLAYTON: Well gosh. Guess I'll just keep the news about Justin to myself.

NATALIE: Justin? What about him?

CLAYTON: Oh no. You're not interested.

JAMES: That's what you said.

NATALIE: Tell me or I'll push you in the pool. *(NATALIE lunges at CLAYTON.)* Help me, Mina. *(MINA crosses to help.)*

MINA: Gladly!

CLAYTON: OK. OK! Justin's on his way to the party.

NATALIE: This party? Tonight? Did he call? When?!

JAMES: When?

NATALIE: Yes!

JAMES: *(Teasing her mercilessly.)* Clayton, when would you say when?

CLAYTON: When? When what?

NATALIE: I don't know which one of you to kill first.

MINA: You guys are mean.

NATALIE: Tell me!

JAMES and CLAYTON: *(Using robot voices.)* Ten minutes ago.

NATALIE: So when's he coming?

JAMES and CLAYTON: *(Using robot voices.)* Our computer says... *(Checking their watches at the same time.)* right now!

NATALIE: What?!! I gotta get out of this bathing suit. *(NATALIE is rushing around trying to find her clothes and bag.)*

JAMES: Wait. You've got a crush on this guy, he's on his way over, and you're taking *off* your suit to put on clothes? What's wrong with this picture?

MINA: You look great in your suit.

NATALIE: And so does a cow! *(Pushing JAMES out of the way.)* James, move! I've got to find some shampoo. Where are my clothes? Where did I put them? Find them, Mina. Now!

MINA: Where'd you put them?

NATALIE: If I knew that, I wouldn't be asking you to look for them.

JAMES: *(Imitating NATALIE.)* Don't you know anything, Mina?

NATALIE: Look. I'm going in here to wash my hair. You guys keep Justin busy when he gets here. Don't let him leave. Say nice things about me.

CLAYTON: I promised never to tell a lie.

NATALIE: *(Exasperated.)* I need new friends.

MINA: *(Puzzled, a little hurt.)* Natalie!

NATALIE: Look, I'll be out in a second. Mina, try to be useful for once and find my clothes! *(NATALIE goes into the changing room/rest room, slamming the door.)*

JAMES: Man, she's mean when she's wet.

CLAYTON: I thought this was a good hiding place, Mina.

MINA: Thanks.

CLAYTON: Let's go back up to the party. We're gonna be reported as missing!

MINA: I better stay here.

JAMES: Mina's got her orders. Wouldn't want to cross the boss.

MINA: Natalie's not my boss!

(JAMES is looking around the bathhouse.)

CLAYTON: Come on. I brought all my best CDs. We could dance or something.

MINA: I —

CLAYTON: Don't hang around here just so she can yell at you again. Let's go!

MINA: I want to, but I've gotta find —

JAMES: *(Holding up the backpack with NATALIE's clothes.)* This?

MINA: *(Crossing to him to take it.)* You found her clothes! Thanks, James —

JAMES: *(Holding the backpack out of her reach.)* Not so fast. Not so fast. We have an opportunity here.

MINA: James. She's gonna be done any minute. She'll need her clothes.

JAMES: Exactly. And I've got them.

CLAYTON: James, you are brilliant!

MINA: What are you thinking? You wouldn't — James!

JAMES: Watch me. *(JAMES begins to hide her backpack in the bathhouse.)*

CLAYTON: *(Imitating NATALIE.)* "Hey Justin. Hope you like the natural look."
(The boys laugh.)

MINA: This is just great. Look, I'm the one she's gonna kill.

JAMES: Tell her you looked for them, but couldn't find them. Tell her anything.

CLAYTON: Who cares what you tell her! This is your chance! Get her back. Don't you get sick of how she treats you?

MINA: But she's my friend.

NATALIE: *(Calling from inside the shower.)* Mina? Mina! Ga, is there anyone any slower than you?
(MINA pauses for a moment. She then rushes to where JAMES has hidden the backpack.)

MINA: Bury it. *(She shoves more stuff on top of NATALIE's backpack.)*

CLAYTON and JAMES: All right, Mina.
(All three exchange high-fives.)

NATALIE: *(Opening the door. She is wrapped in a towel.)* Mina! *(Seeing the boys.)* Could you guys please be gentlemen and leave. *(JAMES and CLAYTON sit down at the same time.)* Did you skip sixth grade English? Please leave! You've got a job to do. Go talk to Justin. *(They just smile at her.)* Stop looking at me! Mina. Give me my clothes. *(MINA doesn't move.)* Mina!

MINA: They're...lost.

NATALIE: What?

MINA: Lost.

NATALIE: How could they be lost?

MINA: Maybe someone took them. I don't know. They're just lost.

NATALIE: Did you look for them? Really look for them.

MINA: Yes.

(JAMES and CLAYTON begin to snicker — trying not to laugh.)

NATALIE: I'm sure this is all very funny to you.

JAMES: Not at all!

CLAYTON: Are we laughing? *(They are.)*

NATALIE: You are really enjoying this, aren't you. All of you! *(The boys are really laughing now.)* Why don't you just leave. Get out! Leave! This isn't funny! It's not funny!! *(NATALIE is starting to cry.)* Leave! Just... leave... *(NATALIE sits, defeated.)*

JAMES: OK, boss. We are leaving!

CLAYTON: See *all* of you at the party, Natalie. Come on, Mina. Let's go dance!

MINA: OK.

JAMES: Outta here!

(The boys exit, laughing. MINA starts to go with them but she stops. NATALIE is sitting, no longer crying, but very still, quiet. MINA crosses back into the bathhouse.)

MINA: Natalie —

NATALIE: Why'd you do it?

MINA: What?

NATALIE: Be just like all the others.

MINA: What are you talking about?

NATALIE: All my other friends would start out nice, too. Then they always turn on me. I thought you were different.

MINA: We were just kidding around.

NATALIE: Oh.

MINA: Just having fun. *(MINA crosses slowly to where the backpack is hidden. She pulls it out, and sets it down next to NATALIE.)* It was a joke.

NATALIE: Yeah.

(NATALIE just lets the backpack sit next to her. She doesn't pick it up or move. MINA looks at NATALIE for a moment, then exits. NATALIE sits silently.)

End of Scene.

Natural Selection

CHARACTERS: (4 w)
    Shannon, 11–12
    Tanisha, 11–12
    Marty, 11–12
    Angela, 11–12

SETTING:
    A hiking trail in a state park

ANGELA, MARTY, TANISHA, and SHANNON, all 11-12, are kids from the suburbs who have been bused to a state park for a day. MARTY is the leader of their group, which is supposed to be studying the rock formations in the park for school. As the scene begins, the girls are finishing a race down a hiking trail.

(SHANNON runs on, tosses her backpack off and sits on the ground.)

TANISHA: *(Offstage.)* Shannon!

MARTY: *(Offstage.)* Wait up, Shannon!

    (TANISHA and MARTY burst on stage. They are breathless. TANISHA collapses dramatically.)

SHANNON: You made it.

MARTY: Barely!

SHANNON: Wasn't that an incredible hiking trail?

MARTY: So why didn't we *hike* it?

SHANNON: It's more fun to run.

TANISHA: More fun for you! I'm sure I twisted my ankle.

MARTY: You'll live.

TANISHA: No, really. It's broken. I'm sure it is.

SHANNON: And is your tail bone still bruised from the bus ride?

TANISHA: Yes! All those bumpy country roads. Why didn't they tell us they were taking us half-way around the world?

MARTY: We're just fifteen miles from school.

SHANNON: This is a great park! I've been coming to this park since I was a kid.

TANISHA: Where do you get something to eat around here? I'm hungry.

SHANNON: (*Coming toward her with berries.*) These berries are edible.

TANISHA: (*Jumping up.*) Get that nature stuff away from me.

MARTY: It's a miracle. She can walk!

TANISHA: But it still hurts! No more racing, Shannon.

SHANNON: I'm in training. (*She runs around MARTY and TANISHA.*) Soccer star! She makes the goal. (*The other two girls just look at her.*) OK, let's get down to business. What rock formations did we pass, captain?

MARTY: All I saw were my feet. I was trying not to trip. (*ANGELA enters, very breathless, behind the other girls. She hangs back, trying to catch her breath, before joining the group.*)

MARTY: We're gonna have to do that trail again, guys. We were supposed to see (*Pulling out a school paper.*) "bear rock," whatever that is.

TANISHA: Wasn't that the one made outta limestone or something that the Indians named?

ANGELA: It was right past the top of the ridge.

MARTY: Angela!

SHANNON: I thought you'd given out on the home stretch.

ANGELA: I just took my time.

TANISHA: You were smart.

SHANNON: She was scared! She never likes to race. She doesn't play soccer —

MARTY: So?

ANGELA: I'm not interested in games!

TANISHA: That's not want Andrew said.

SHANNON: Gossip! Let's hear it!

ANGELA: I don't know what she's talking about.

TANISHA: Does "Spin the Bottle" at JJ's party ring any bells?

ANGELA: Oh, that. Sure, I'll play *that* game.

MARTY: You will?

ANGELA: It's no big deal. You just kiss.

SHANNON: It'd be a big deal for Marty.

TANISHA: First time! First time!

MARTY: I've been kissed!

TANISHA: By your mother!

ANGELA: Lay off her, guys. Ga, you're so immature.

MARTY: Yeah! Thanks, Angela.

SHANNON: So who's got the map?

MARTY: I do. I'm the captain.

SHANNON: Then tell us where we're supposed to go next.

MARTY: *(Reading.)* "Find four examples of fossils on the cliffs leading toward the river. Do rubbings of them for your geology notebooks."

TANISHA: I'm not climbing out on any cliffs.

SHANNON: Up them! We climb up them!

TANISHA: Say what?

SHANNON: Don't worry, you just find a little ledge in the rock for your feet, and then you pull yourself up with your hands.

TANISHA: And pigs will fly next Sunday. You're not gonna catch me doin' that.

SHANNON: You need to build up some arm strength. Here's your chance. *(SHANNON drops to the ground and starts to do push-ups.)* Warm-ups!

MARTY: *I'm* the captain! Warm-ups! *(She begins to do push-ups.)* Fall in everybody.

TANISHA: I'd dislocate my shoulder if I did even two of those. And pull out my back.

MARTY: Then try *one*.

ANGELA: Tanisha, can't you do anything?

TANISHA: I don't see you sweatin'!

ANGELA: *I* am looking for fossils. (*She turns away from the group, and she begins to look around.*)

TANISHA: All right. But just one.

(*SHANNON and MARTY stop to watch TANISHA try a push up.*)

TANISHA: You sure this isn't poison ivy or something?

SHANNON: One!

(*TANISHA gets on the ground.*)

MARTY: All right!

(*TANISHA is just pushing herself up, groaning loudly, when ANGELA cries out.*)

ANGELA: Oh my gosh. Look!

MARTY: What?

ANGELA: It's a bird. I think it's hurt.

(*The other three girls cross to where ANGELA is bending down.*)

TANISHA: Where?

ANGELA: See.

MARTY: It's so small.

SHANNON: It's a baby. It's been pushed out of its nest.

TANISHA: How do you know?

ANGELA: Look at its wing. It's broken.

SHANNON: No. I think it was born like that.

TANISHA: Who made you the nature queen?

SHANNON: I told you! I've been coming here all my life. I saw something like this before with my Mom. She said sometimes birds are born with wings that don't work. They're deformed. The mother bird sees that, so she pushes the baby out of the nest.

ANGELA: That's cruel.

SHANNON: She knows that it will never survive. So why feed it?

TANISHA: Glad my Momma didn't do that to me.

MARTY: We can't just leave it here.

ANGELA: Let's put it back in its nest. Maybe if the Mom thinks the baby flew back up, she'll want to take care of it.

MARTY: Yeah.

SHANNON: If we touch it, she'll smell us.

TANISHA: I don't smell.

SHANNON: We've got a human smell. So she'll reject it again anyway.

TANISHA: Then let's take it back with us. Bet we'd be the only team to come back with something alive.

ANGELA: Barely alive. Look at it. It looks so scared.

TANISHA: I've got a bandanna in my backpack. We could carry it in that. Mrs. Jeniski would let us keep it as a class project, wouldn't she?

ANGELA: Sure she would. We could feed it. It wouldn't have to fly if it lived in our class.

SHANNON: This isn't a parakeet or something. It's a wild bird. It won't like living in a cage.

TANISHA: It's better than dying.

SHANNON: I'm not so sure.

TANISHA: What do you mean?

ANGELA: Just because this little bird isn't strong, just because it isn't the best one in the nest, you can't relate to it, Shannon.

TANISHA: Soccer star.

SHANNON: We're not talking about me!

ANGELA: No, we're talking about a defenseless little bird!

SHANNON: Who was born wrong! Nature didn't mean for it to survive.

MARTY: Maybe we could leave it here, go do our fossil rubbings, then see if it's still here when we get back.

ANGELA: That's easy. Leave it, and hope it's gone, so we don't have to make a choice.

MARTY: Have you got a better idea?

ANGELA: I said my idea. Put it back in the nest.

SHANNON: Where it will die.

TANISHA: So what's your idea, Shannon, since you know so much.

SHANNON: It's suffering. See.

ANGELA: Oh, look how it's breathing. Poor thing.

SHANNON: I think we should put it out of it's misery.

MARTY: You mean kill it?

SHANNON: Yes.

ANGELA: No!

TANISHA: I couldn't kill anything.

SHANNON: But it's suffering. It's going to die anyway. I hate to see anything suffer.

ANGELA: I say we take it back.

TANISHA: Me, too. We know what you want, Shannon.

ANGELA: Marty? You're the captain. What do we do?

MARTY: I don't know.

(All four girls are silent for a moment, looking at the bird.)

TANISHA: I thought this day was gonna be about rocks. Not about life and death.

ANGELA: I wish they'd never brought us here.

(They sit in silence again.)

SHANNON: We've got thirty minutes. Then we're supposed to be back at the bus.

TANISHA: With fossil rubbings.

(They are silent again.)

MARTY: I say, we try — try, anyway, to help it live. I don't want to leave something to die. Or make it die. OK, Shannon?

SHANNON: You're the captain.

MARTY: Let's go.

End of Scene.

Two-on-Two

CHARACTERS: (4 m)
   Jay, 12
   Malachi, 12
   Raymond, 14
   Tre, 14

SETTING:
   A basketball court at a public playground

JAY, 12, is practicing basketball moves on the court. His friend, MALACHI, 12, enters. He is talking on his cell phone, which was a present from his Dad. Actors will enjoy how the playing of basketball in the scene changes from something fun to something threatening.

MALACHI: All right. I heard you.

JAY: Get off your fancy phone, man.

MALACHI: *(Motioning him to leave him alone.)* Don't worry. I'll be home by five.

JAY: *(Dribbling noisily around him.)* Who you talkin' to?

MALACHI: *(Turning away from JAY.)* What was that? OK. I won't forget. Bye.

JAY: *(Tossing him the ball.)* Think fast, Mr. Cell-phone! One-on-one. Come on.

MALACHI: *(Flopping down on a bench.)* Not today, Jay. I need some rest.

JAY: You look like what the dog dragged in. What happened to you?

MALACHI: I'm tired, man.

JAY: From what? Your Daddy keep you up with some all-night preachin'?

MALACHI: I went to Leslie's birthday party.

JAY: Was that last night?

MALACHI: I called to see if you wanted to roll with me. But you were nowhere to be found.

JAY: Aww, I had to go to my aunt's. Dag, I can't believe I missed that party. Did Leslie look good?

MALACHI: You know she did.

JAY: And Aleesha?

MALACHI: Even better.

JAY: Better than the birthday girl?

MALACHI: Depends on your taste.

JAY: What are you talkin' about! You won't be tastin' a thing till you grow some more.

MALACHI: I was just checkin' out the sights —

JAY: Dancin' with that girl gave her a sight — right over the top of your head! Where you come up to, Leslie's waist?

MALACHI: I didn't go there to dance.

JAY: Your Daddy let you dance?

MALACHI: Don't give me any of that. I can do what I want.

JAY: But you gotta watch your step. I was there, remember? Your Daddy got up in front of the whole congregation. *(JAY jumps dramatically up onto a bench, and does a good-natured imitation of MALACHI's father.)* "Brothers and sisters, I am askin' for your help in the raisin' of my son Malachi. If any one of you see him steppin' out of line, I ask you to pull him back in. Say Amen."

MALACHI: I'm walkin' the line.

JAY: "I ask you to be my boy's guardian angel. To watch over him as one of your own. I say, say Amen!"

MALACHI: *(Enjoying his friend's imitation.)* Amen!
(RAYMOND and TRE have entered, and have overheard JAY's sermon.)

RAYMOND: Amen!

TRE: Alleluia.

JAY: Hey Raymond. Tre. You guys were there that Sunday, weren't you?

RAYMOND: Wasn't there. But heard the word. We all got to look out for our Malachi, right?

JAY: Right!

TRE: Gotta do what we gotta do *(Singing to the tune of "Jesus Loves Me.")* 'cause his Daddy asked us to.

MALACHI: You dissin' my Dad?

RAYMOND: No. No disrespect intended.

MALACHI: He's a good man.

TRE: That's why he wants to have a good boy.

JAY: *(Jumping up, trying to get a game going.)* All right. Two-on-two. You look like you're recovered, Malachi. Let's take 'em on.

RAYMOND: Recovered from bein' out all night somewhere you're not supposed to be?

MALACHI: What're you talkin' about?

TRE: Leslie's place is off limits to a boy like you.

MALACHI: My Dad knew I was goin' there.

RAYMOND: Yeah, but does he know that Leslie's brother is one of the biggest dealers in the game?

MALACHI: What? You're crazy.

RAYMOND: You don't believe me? You disrespecting me now?

JAY: No, he's —

RAYMOND: Let him answer for himself.

MALACHI: I'm... surprised.

RAYMOND: Well, wake up and smell the reality.

MALACHI: Come on, Jay. Let's go talk to Leslie. I wanna check this out for myself.

RAYMOND: *(Cutting him off.)* Not so fast. You got the proof right in your pocket.

MALACHI: What are you talking about?

TRE: Have a look.

(*MALACHI reaches into his jacket pocket. He pulls out a bag of a few rocks of crack.*)

MALACHI: Crack! How did this get here? This isn't mine!

RAYMOND: You're right about that. It's mine. Thank you, delivery boy. It's just what I ordered.

TRE: The preacher-boy is running drugs. What will his father say!

MALACHI: I'm not! Somebody put these in my pocket. I didn't have anything to do with this.

RAYMOND: Jay, didn't you see him take those rocks out of his pocket?

JAY: (*Frightened.*) Yeah.

MALACHI: Jay!!

RAYMOND: And didn't he go to Leslie's house last night?

JAY: Yeah.

TRE: Doesn't take a special investigator to put two and two together. Looks like you've taken on a new job, preacher-boy!

RAYMOND: Now, if we are to keep the pledge we made to your father —

MALACHI: You didn't make any pledge —

TRE: It takes a village to raise a child.

RAYMOND: And we're the chiefs!

MALACHI: I'm gettin' out of here —
(*MALACHI tries to push his way past RAYMOND, but RAYMOND grabs his shoulders and pushes him back. There is a tense, silent standoff among the boys.*)

MALACHI: What do you want?

RAYMOND: We just wanna keep you outta trouble with your Daddy. And right now, you're in a bad way. Partyin' at a dealer's house. Drugs in your pocket.

JAY: He's right, Malachi.

RAYMOND: Oh, yeah, and we got a witness on our side. (*Pointing to a frightened JAY.*)

TRE: But tell you what. We won't tell your preacher-Daddy a thing if you just keep the lines going.

MALACHI: Huh?

RAYMOND: Since Leslie's your little girlfriend, it's a lot easier for you to go visitin' her house than me. I'm not too welcome in that neighborhood. Seen some trouble over there.

TRE: But Leslie's brother's got stuff that we want. And you're gonna keep gettin' it for us, just like you did last night.

JAY: Do what he says, Malachi.

(The older boys begin to circle MALACHI, passing the basketball threateningly around him on their lines. MALACHI has to dodge the ball.)

TRE: Get us the stuff.

RAYMOND: Or what will your father say!

TRE: Think fast!

JAY: Just do it!

RAYMOND: Get over there.

TRE: Get us more!

RAYMOND: Get over there. Now!

(RAYMOND roughly tosses the ball to MALACHI. He catches it, but it knocks him to the ground.)

MALACHI: Yeah. I'll go.

(RAYMOND and TRE begin to exit, then stop.)

RAYMOND: Oh. You wanna keep a piece of this? Call it the first step into the business. *(He tosses a tiny rock of crack to MALACHI, who catches it.)* This way, Jay.

(JAY and MALACHI exchange a look. JAY is drawn by his friend, but he is more afraid of the older boys. He leaves with them.)

MALACHI: *(To himself.)* I'll go. I'll go as far away from you as I can. *(Tossing down the crack, he pulls out his cell phone.)* Dad? Dad. I gotta talk to you. Now.

End of Scene.

The Bigger Picture

Characters (2 m, 2 w)
    Tia (w), 12
    Zayd (m), 12
    Dean (m), 12
    Nadia (w), 12

SETTING:
A study room in a middle school library

TIA, ZAYD, DEAN, and NADIA are all good friends. They have started a magazine, Starbright, as a project for their science class. TIA is helping ZAYD with an article he is finishing up for the magazine. They are sitting in front of a computer terminal in their school library.

TIA: These pictures are incredible, Zayd. Did you download them?

ZAYD: From the NASA web site. You can get photos of the shuttle, pictures of Mars —

TIA: And we can publish them in our magazine, no problem?

ZAYD: These photos belong to us cause we're Americans.

TIA: *(Proudly.)* I'm Hispanic-American —

ZAYD: And I'm Armenian-American. OK? We're all "something-American," but we still get these pictures.

TIA: Why?

ZAYD: The government pays for the space program and our taxes pay for the government. We can print any of these we want!

TIA: That's amazing. Which one should we use for the cover? We want people to really notice our first issue.

ZAYD: Any magazine started by four seventh graders, I think the world will notice.

TIA: Zayd, we're only publishing twenty copies for our science class.

ZAYD: Today, our middle school, tomorrow, the world. You gotta think big, Tia.

(DEAN and NADIA enter.)

DEAN: Attention *Starbright* magazine staff!

ZAYD: Hey, Dean, check these out.

NADIA: He said "Attention."

TIA: And he's the executive editor.

DEAN: Thanks, Tia. Big news. *(To NADIA.)* Drum roll, please.

(NADIA does a drum roll on a desk with her hands.)

DEAN: We got invited.

TIA: To what?

NADIA: On the field trip. With the eighth graders!

ZAYD: You mean it?

DEAN: Mr. Preston said of all the kids in the seventh grade, we got picked to do the science museum overnight. *(Imitating the teacher.)* "Your starting of *Starbright* magazine shows your exceptional interest in space." So we get to go! *Party!!*

ZAYD: All right!

NADIA: We take a bus to the city, spend all day Friday in the museum, spend the night in a hotel, then get all of Saturday for shopping! Tia, what should we wear?

TIA: I don't know —

ZAYD: *(Cutting her off.)* I'll shoot hundreds of shots for the magazine of our whole staff in front of a space capsule—

NADIA: *(Posing.)* All four of us!

ZAYD: Then we'll pose in front of a vintage aircraft. Tia, you can cover the human interest angles, like: *(Using a scientific voice.)* "How does it feel when you consider the

advances humankind has made in air and space travel" —
wait. What am I talking about, I can't go.

NADIA and DEAN: What??

ZAYD: I forgot! I'm grounded.

TIA: Till when?

ZAYD: Next month.

NADIA: What'd you do? Rob a bank?

ZAYD: I messed up my literature grade, and my math, and
history.

TIA: *That's* why you wouldn't let me see your report card.

ZAYD: My parents are really mad. They say I play around on
the internet instead of studying.

TIA: They're right!

NADIA: But this trip was given to the entire *Starbright* staff.
You've gotta come, Zayd. We need a strategy — a strategy to convince your parents to let you go.

ZAYD: Yeah, and I'm gonna be the first kid to fly to the moon
tomorrow.

DEAN: We'll come up with something. Here. You know
Zayd's Mom, right, Tia?

TIA: Sure.

DEAN: Then you pretend to be her. I'll be his Dad. Nadia,
you coach. (*Pretending to be the Dad.*) "Hello, son.
Anything exciting happen at school today?"

ZAYD: (*To NADIA.*) Should I say yes?

NADIA: Yes.

ZAYD: (*To DEAN.*) Yes.

TIA: Then tell us.

ZAYD: Well, I got this big honor.

DEAN and TIA: Oh?!

ZAYD: I got asked to go on an eighth grade field trip.

DEAN: How wonderful. You go right ahead, son!

NADIA: Dean, you're no help. Get up. I'll be the Dad. "Son,

if you want to go on this trip, you're going to have to earn our trust again."

DEAN: Man, I hate it when my Dad says that.

NADIA: "You are too old to let anything get in the way of your school work."

ZAYD: But not old enough to do what I want! Why am I too old for some things, but not old enough for others, huh, Dad?

NADIA: *(As Dad.)* "Because you're twelve. Deal with it."

TIA: *(As Mom.)* "It's important for you to work very hard in school. How else are you going to be a success in this life."

ZAYD: Please, can I go?

TIA: *(As Mom.)* "Well…"

DEAN: She's giving in. Now's the time to promise to do something really helpful around the house, or go somewhere she's been trying to drag you to for months —

NADIA: Or promise to take your sister to the park on Saturday —

ZAYD: No way.

TIA: Or take out the garbage —

ZAYD: I do.

DEAN: Then try looking really sweetly at your Mom. Give her a hug. That always works for me.

NADIA: I know. Tell her you'll get off the phone right when she asks you next time.

TIA: *(Teasing him.)* And tell her you'll not get mad when she calls you "pumpkin" in front of your friends.

DEAN: She calls you "pumpkin?"

ZAYD: Lay off!

DEAN: *(As Mom.)* "Bye, 'pumpkin,' have a good day at school!"

ZAYD: I thought we were working on my strategy!

NADIA: I got it! Here, I'll be you. You be your Dad. *(They switch places.)* "Dad?" *(As herself.)* Make sure you're not slouching or anything.

TIA: That makes my Mom crazy, too.

NADIA: *(Sitting up very straight, as ZAYD.)* "Dad. I promise, if you let me go on this trip, I will strive to live up to each and every expectation you have of me for the rest of my life."

ZAYD: Isn't that a little extreme?

NADIA: It'll make a point.

TIA: Zayd, just say, "I messed up. I'm sorry. I'm working to do better." They'll let you go.

DEAN: I don't know. That sounds too honest.

ZAYD: It's not like I'm asking to go to an amusement park or something, right?

DEAN: Right. You don't have to tell them about the parties we'll be havin' behind the chaperones' backs.

NADIA: Or what might happen on the bus when I get to sit next to Damion —

DEAN: *(Teasing her.)* From the eighth grade!

ZAYD: I mean, this trip is going to help our science grade, right?

DEAN and NADIA: Right!

DEAN: Your parents will cave, Zayd. No problem!

ZAYD: Thanks, guys. Now we can plan out our stories, Tia. We can fill ten issues of *Starbright* with everything we're gonna see.

TIA: I've got a better idea. I'll be the home-base link for the trip. You guys can e-mail me here in the library, and I'll start working on stories from here.

NADIA: What?

TIA: I can get us ahead on our second issue while you guys do the on-site reporting —

ZAYD: Don't you want to come?

(TIA does not reply.)

NADIA: This trip is for all of us.

DEAN: Are you grounded too? Here, let me be your Mom. "Welcome home, Tianita."

NADIA: I'll be you. "Ola, Mom. I get to go to the science museum."

ZAYD: She wants you to be a doctor, right. This will help!

NADIA: *(As TIA.)* "And I'll write all these great stories for *Starbright,* my magazine. You can read them —"

TIA: She can't read them, OK?

(The group is silent for a moment.)

ZAYD: Then you read them to her. In Spanish. And the pictures are cool —

TIA: That's not the point. Look, I promised my Mom I would never miss a day of school, not for anything.

DEAN: But this is *like* school.

TIA: Which part? The party in the hotel or playing musical chairs on the bus until Nadia gets to sit next to Damion? Sure. I'd like to go. But I keep my promises to my Mother.

NADIA: But it's just a day.

TIA: A day when I would miss school, then not be home to help with my sisters before my Mom goes to work —

NADIA: Get somebody else to baby-sit. I'm gonna get my aunt to watch my brothers.

DEAN: Tia, if you need to borrow some money for it —

TIA: I don't need money. I need to stay here to go to school and to be with my Mom. Saturdays are the only time I have more than one hour a day with her. All the other days, I go to school, then she goes to work. Don't you get it? I want to be with her.

ZAYD: More than you want to do *Starbright?*

TIA: Yes.

NADIA: Wow.

DEAN: I don't know too many kids who like their mothers.

NADIA: We're still friends, though, right? Still the *Starbright* staff?

TIA: Of course. OK. Let's get this cover designed. It's our first issue, so we want — sorry, Dean. You're the executive editor. This is your job.

DEAN: Maybe it should be yours.

(TIA and DEAN exchange a look of new understanding of each other. TIA crosses to the computer.)

TIA: Zayd, bring up the photos. Have a look, team. I like the one that's looking way off into space. Into the future.

(The students gather around the computer monitor.)

End of Scene.

The Game   Adapted from *Round Pegs Square Pegs*

CHARACTERS: (4, any combination of m and/or w)
    Big Round
    Small Round
    Small Square
    Big Square

SETTING:

Where the game is played in a divided world

Round Pegs, Square Pegs is fantasy set in a world controlled by two superpowers — the Rounds and the Squares. The set for the original production looked like a giant game board, divided down the middle, with a spinner at the center. Upstage was a huge abacus, on which there were "odd-beads" — beads of different shapes and colors. Both the Rounds and the Squares want to win the odd-beads over to their side of the game. The SMALLS of both worlds are the pawns in what becomes a very dangerous game, because the BIGS back up their contests and threats with "peg-power." Round Pegs, Square Pegs is a metaphor for our fractured world, and the pegs represent the nuclear arsenal that remains a deadly threat. This play was written to give young people a sense of empowerment in the face of an enormous challenge — to bring about a peaceful world. In this play, the SMALLS ultimately rearrange their world, stand up for their future and thereby make peace.

In this scene, SMALL ROUND is preparing to spin in the Great Game for the first time.

BIG ROUND: Small Round, the game will begin soon.

SMALL ROUND: Ready!

BIG ROUND: You have been selected, from all the Small Rounds, to spin in the Great Game. You should be very proud.

SMALL ROUND: I've been practicing.

BIG ROUND: Remember, you begin by standing in the center. And then you must join hands with one of them!

SMALL ROUND: Them?

BIG ROUND: A Square!

SMALL ROUND: *(With wicked anticipation.)* A Square!

BOTH. Wicked, horrid, awful Square.
Come and get us if you dare.
We will show you who's the strongest.
We've been in control the longest.

SMALL ROUND: Ooo, I can't wait to see a Square. Do they really have square heads and no hearts?

BIG ROUND: They certainly do.

SMALL ROUND: They've probably got big teeth, big fangs that they go around chewing up Rounds with.

BIG ROUND: Squares do not appear evil or terrible — on the outside.

SMALL ROUND: I bet I'll be bigger and stronger than Small Square. I can win if we fight. I know I can.

BIG ROUND: The object of today's game is not to fight, Small Round, only to win. Now make sure your Round hat is sitting roundly on your head. Let's hear your pledge.

SMALL ROUND: *(Accompanied by Round hand movements.)*
Rounds win with the top.
Always go, never stop.
Turning, spinning. Always right.
Out of mind, out of sight.

BIG ROUND: Excellent. Now keep pledging. I must make sure all is in order before the game begins.

SMALL ROUND: I'll stay right here and pledge.

BIG ROUND: *(Turns to leave, but stops.)* Small Round?

SMALL ROUND: Yes, Big Round?

BIG ROUND: You do know that we play this game so that you and all the Small Rounds will have a Round world to live and play in.

SMALL ROUND: That's what you've said, Big Round.

BIG ROUND: Good. All right. Pledge.

(BIG ROUND exits.)

SMALL ROUND: *(Quite loudly so BIG ROUND can hear him.)*
Rounds win with the top.
Always go, never stop.
Turning… Spinning… Turning… Spinning… *(SMALL ROUND becomes interested in his toy, his "ro-ho," a kind of cup and ball toy.)* Ro-ho, boom. Ro-ho *(He tries to do a trick with it.)* Ro-ho, double Round pow!
(It doesn't work. SMALL SQUARE has entered from his side, and watches SMALL ROUND curiously.)

SMALL ROUND: Oh, come on. Maybe if I try it this way.

SMALL SQUARE: Hold it the other way.

SMALL ROUND: What way?

SMALL SQUARE: Straighter. *(The SMALLS' eyes meet. They freeze.)* Are you?

SMALL ROUND: Are you?

SMALL SQUARE: A Round?

SMALL ROUND: A Square!!

SMALL SQUARE: *(At the same time as SMALL ROUND.)*
Wicked, horrid, awful Round
With great evil you abound.
We will show you who's the strongest
We've been in control the longest.

SMALL ROUND: *(At the same time as SMALL SQUARE.)*

Wicked horrid awful Square
Come and get us if you dare.
We will show you who's the strongest.
We've been in control the longest.

SMALL ROUND: Get out of here.

SMALL SQUARE: You.

SMALL ROUND: I'm supposed to be here.

SMALL SQUARE: So am I. For the Game.

SMALL ROUND: So am I.

SMALL SQUARE: So?

SMALL ROUND: So. So!

(Stand off. They look at one another cautiously.)

SMALL ROUND: What's that supposed to be on your head?

SMALL SQUARE: What?

SMALL ROUND: That?

SMALL SQUARE: My Small Square hat. What's that supposed to be on *your* head?

SMALL ROUND: My Small Round Hat. Once I get big, I'll wear it over my eyes like Big Round. You can see better that way.

SMALL SQUARE: When I get big, I'll wear my Small Square hat over my eyes, too. All the Big Squares have one.

SMALL ROUND: And you've all got a make-Square gun, that you shoot Rounds with to change them into Squares, don't you.

SMALL SQUARE: We do not.

SMALL ROUND: You're just hiding it. All Squares are cheats.

SMALL SQUARE: All Rounds are stupid. You've got little round marbles in you head instead of brains.

SMALL ROUND: We do not. I've got a brain just like you do. *(He/she catches him/herself. An awkward pause.)* Except it's bigger. Rounds are smarter than Squares.

SMALL SQUARE: Then how come you can't figure out how to make your Square-bare work?

SMALL ROUND: My what?

SMALL SQUARE: Your Square-bare. Your toy!

SMALL ROUND: That's my Ro-ho.

SMALL SQUARE: Oh.

SMALL ROUND: *(Patronizingly.)* "Ro-ho." Understand.

SMALL SQUARE: It's just like my square-bare.

SMALL ROUND: Nothing of mine is like anything of yours, OK, wicked, horrid, awful Square?

SMALL SQUARE: Fine.

SMALL ROUND: Yeah. Fine.

SMALL SQUARE: Yeah.

SMALL ROUND: Sure.

SMALL SQUARE: Sure.

SMALL ROUND: Fine!

(Stand off.)

SMALL ROUND: Big Round said the Squares are gonna try and take over all the odd-beads on the abacus. But we'll win the game.

SMALL SQUARE: Big Square said the same thing about the Rounds. Big Square is always right.

SMALL ROUND: Big Round is always right. So you must be wrong.

SMALL SQUARE: That's what you think.

SMALL ROUND: Rounds aren't supposed to think. So there.

SMALL SQUARE: There. *(Pause.)* You're not supposed to think? Really?

SMALL ROUND: We don't need to think, because we are Rounds. Rounds naturally know what's right. And we've got the peg-power to prove it.

SMALL SQUARE: *(Timidly.)* I know.

SMALL ROUND: What's the matter, Small Square. You scared of a little peg-power?

SMALL SQUARE: No.

(SMALL ROUND begins to stalk SMALL SQUARE, enjoying

finding what is apparently a sensitive subject with SMALL SQUARE.)

SMALL ROUND: *(Makes a whistling missile sound, then the sound of an explosion.)* KABOOM!!

SMALL SQUARE: Cut it out.

SMALL ROUND: *(With a big gesture.)* BBOOOOOOM!!

SMALL SQUARE: That's enough! *(He runs off, exits.)*

SMALL ROUND: *(Calling after him.)* Come on, I was just playing. Stupid, scaredy-cat Square. *(He picks up his toy.)* This isn't a Square bare. *(Imitating SMALL SQUARE.)* "Try holding it the other way, straighter." Right! *(He does so, and the toy works.)* Hey!
(Suddenly BIG ROUND and BIG SQUARE enter. SMALL SQUARE follows behind BIG SQUARE. The two BIGS meet in the center. SMALLS play "Hail to the Chief" on kazoos. The BIGS extend their hands toward the other. They shake hands with a jerky one-two-three motion.)

BIG ROUND: Welcome, Big Square.

BIG SQUARE: Big Round, welcome.

BIG ROUND: Today we come together —

BIG SQUARE: Together come we —

BIG ROUND: Today, to divide the remaining odd-beads on the Great Abacus.

BIG SQUARE: Those wickedly different —

BIG ROUND: Funny colored —

BOTH BIGS: Odd-beads!

BIG SQUARE: The Great Abacus's odd-beads have long been a point of discussion —

BIG ROUND: Of competition.

BIG SQUARE: Of contest.

BIG ROUND: Of...
(Both BIGS point quickly to their well-trained SMALLS to fill in the blank.)

SMALLS: Conflict!

BIG SQUARE: Between our two worlds.

BIG ROUND: Right now, the beads which are round —

BIG SQUARE: And the beads which are square are —

BOTH BIGS: Evenly divided.

(Tense pause.)

BIG ROUND: Let us begin the game now to divide the rest.

BIG SQUARE: But first review the rules, if you think best.

BIG ROUND: Why certainly, friend Square. It's a very simple game. Every time we play it, the rules are the same.

BIG SQUARE: Small Square?

BIG ROUND: Small Round?

BOTH BIGS: To the center of the game.

(The SMALLS cross to the spinner at the center of the board. They act out the motions as the BIGS describe them.)

BIG SQUARE: The Smalls go to the center and are spun like a top. And we count the times they turn before they stop.

BIG ROUND: Then we see which way they've landed toward Round or Square, which decides who takes the odd-beads, fair and square.

BIG SQUARE: If they land toward a Square, after spinning four times, then the Squares get four odd-beads, which happens most times.

BIG ROUND: Not always! Rounds have gotten six beads from one spin.

BIG SQUARE: Come on, six are easy. Squares have gotten ten.

BIG ROUND: We've both had our victories playing this game. But today's game is special. It's not quite the same.

SMALL SQUARE: Why?

BIGS: *(Ignoring SMALL SQUARE.)* Let's begin.

(The BIGS move toward the center. The SMALLS create the spinner. The BIGS place both hands on the SMALLS.)

BIG ROUND: *(With fake civility.)* Both hands.

BIG SQUARE: Both of us.

BIGS: So it's equal.

> *(The SMALLS spin in a way that first appears fun, but then seems to go out of control.)*

BIGS: One, two, three, four, five, six!

> *(The SMALLS land with a thud, pointing toward SQUARE.)*

BIG SQUARE: Square! There!

BIG ROUND: But the spin wasn't good.

SMALL ROUND: I'll say.

SMALL SQUARE: I'm too dizzy to see.

BIG ROUND: You started with your right hand instead of your knee.

BIG SQUARE: My knee!

BIG ROUND: We agreed. The knee leads the spins, not your hand or your chin.

BIG SQUARE: Well you used your elbow. I saw you that time. Elbows were outlawed in spinning last time.

BIGS: Liar!

BIG ROUND: Do you think I can trust you to remember the rules? You who think Square thoughts you learned in Square Schools!

BIG SQUARE: You Rounds always cheat. There's no trusting you. You make your Round rules to work best for you.

SMALL SQUARE: *(To BIG SQUARE.)* This isn't the game you taught me to play!

BIG SQUARE: What matters now is winning, not the rules or the game.

SMALL ROUND: *(To BIG ROUND.)* But it doesn't seem fair.

BIG ROUND: It never was fair. That's not the point of the game.

BIG SQUARE: *(Holding SMALL SQUARE protectively.)* Big Round. You give me no choice. For the sake of my Small

Square and all of his kind, I must increase my peg-power to protect what is mine.

BIG ROUND: *(Holding SMALL ROUND protectively.)* Feel free, Big Square, do whatever you like. Just remember my Double-X peg if you decide to strike.

BIG SQUARE: *(Exiting angrily.)* Square pegs!

BIG ROUND: *(Exiting angrily.)* Round pegs!

(The SMALLS begin to march off after their BIGS, but they stop, and turn back to one another.)

SMALL ROUND: My ro-ho?

SMALL SQUARE: Yeah?

SMALL ROUND: Holding it the other way and straighter?

SMALL SQUARE: Works?

SMALL ROUND: Yeah.

BIG ROUND: *(Offstage.)* Small Round!

BIG SQUARE: *(Offstage.)* Small Square!

(The SMALLS look at one another, wanting to say more, but they exit quickly.)

End of Scene.

Tea Party in Wonderland

Adapted from *Alice*

CHARACTERS: (1 w, 3 m and/or w)
> Alice, 11–12
> The Mad Hatter
> The March Hare
> The Dormouse

SETTING:
> A tea party in Wonderland

This is the classic scene from Alice *in Wonderland, when ALICE has tea with the MAD HATTER, MARCH HARE, and the forever-sleepy DORMOUSE. In my adaptation, ALICE is a know-it-all preteen whose world is literally turned upside down by her trip to Wonderland. This allows her to see herself from a whole new perspective. In this scene, ALICE is driven to learn more about the Queen who presides over the lovely garden that she spied through a tiny door upon arrival in Wonderland. Her crazed tea-party partners challenge her certainty and move her one step closer to learning from her adventures.*

In the original production, the tea party was set on a huge tablecloth, with most items glued to it. As the scene begins, ALICE is pondering which way to go.

ALICE: The Cheshire Cat said I was to go this way. Or was it that way? Oh, dear, I'm quite turned around.
(Suddenly, the MAD HATTER, MARCH HARE, and the DORMOUSE come rushing on with a huge picnic cloth spread for tea.)

ALICE: A tea party! How lovely. And I am quite hungry.

MAD HATTER and MARCH HARE: *(Singing.)* "Twinkle Twinkle, little bat. How I wonder what you're at." *(They do a crazed dance up and down the tablecloth.)* "Up above the world so high. Like a tea tray in the sky." "Twinkle, twinkle —"

(ALICE sits down.)

MAD HATTER and MARCH HARE: No room!

MARCH HARE: No room!

ALICE: There's plenty of room.

MARCH HARE: Have some wine.

ALICE: I don't see any wine.

MARCH HARE: There isn't any.

(Big laugh from MARCH HARE and MAD HATTER.)

ALICE: Then it wasn't very civil of you to offer it.

MARCH HARE: It wasn't very civil of you to sit down without being invited.

ALICE: You have places for a great many more than three. And I've been walking a long ways, and I thought you might —

MAD HATTER: Your hair wants cutting.

ALICE: Gracious! You should learn not to make personal remarks. It's very rude. And you should hold your teacup thusly —

(ALICE reaches for a teacup, but the MAD HATTER cuts her off.)

MAD HATTER: Why is a raven like a writing desk?

ALICE: Is that a riddle? I believe I can guess that.

MARCH HARE: Do you mean that you can find out the answer to it?

ALICE: Exactly so.

MARCH HARE: Then you should say what you mean.

ALICE: I do! At least I mean what I say — that's the same thing, you know.

MAD HATTER: *(Challenging her.)* Not the same thing a bit. Why you might just as well say that "I see what I eat" is the same thing as "I eat what I see."

MARCH HARE: You might just as well say that "I like what I get" is the same thing as "I get what I like."

DORMOUSE: *(Lifting his head sleepily.)* You might just as well say that "I breathe when I sleep" is the same thing as "I sleep when I breathe."

MAD HATTER: It *is* the same thing with you.

(The DORMOUSE is asleep again.)

ALICE: Words mean what we choose them to mean — nothing more or less. That's what the Cheshire Cat said.

MAD HATTER: Did he!

MARCH HARE: Well!

ALICE: Might I have a piece of cake?

MAD HATTER: What day of the month is it?

ALICE: The fourth.

MAD HATTER: Two days wrong! *(Shaking his broken watch.)* I told you butter wouldn't suit the works.

ALICE: You've put butter in his watch?

MARCH HARE: It was the best butter.

(The MAD HATTER pours tea on the DORMOUSE's nose.)

DORMOUSE: *(Sleepily.)* Of course, of course. Just what I was going to remark myself

ALICE: *(Reaching for a biscuit.)* Butter belongs on biscuits.

MAD HATTER: *(Moving them out of her reach.)* Have you guessed the riddle yet?

ALICE: I give up. What's the answer?

MAD HATTER: I haven't the slightest idea.

MARCH HARE: Nor I.

(They exchange a mad sigh.)

ALICE: Honestly! You might do something better with time than wasting it in asking riddles that have no answers!

MAD HATTER: If you knew Time as well as I do, you wouldn't talk of wasting it. It's *him*.

ALICE: What?

MAD HATTER: I dare say you've never even spoken to Time. If you were on good terms with him, he'd do almost anything you like with the clock.

ALICE: Really? What does Time look like? Do *you* talk to him?

MAD HATTER: Not I!! We quarreled last March, just before he — *(Pointing to the MARCH HARE.)* went mad, you know. It was at a concert, given by the Queen of Hearts.

ALICE: Do you know the queen? I'm longing to meet her.

MARCH HARE: He's sung for the queen!

DORMOUSE: *(Sleepily.)* Twinkle, twinkle, twinkle…

MAD HATTER: *(Singing.)* "Little bat!" You know the song perhaps?

ALICE: I've heard something like it.

MAD HATTER: Well, I'd hardly finished the first verse, when the Queen bawled out, "He's murdering Time! Off with his head."

MARCH HARE: *(Making a mess of 4/4 time)* 1,2,3,4 and 1,2,3,4 —

ALICE: The queen of my garden said that?

MAD HATTER: And ever since he won't do a thing I ask. It's always six o'clock now. *(He looks at his watch.)* Change! *(DORMOUSE, MARCH HARE, and MAD HATTER all get up and run around the tablecloth to new places. ALICE moves now, too.)*

ALICE: *(While racing about.)* Is she so dreadfully savage — the queen, that is?

MAD HATTER: Indeed! But here, it's always six o'clock.

MARCH HARE: Tea time!

MAD HATTER: No time to wash up the things between.

ALICE: Is that why you keep changing places?

(They all sit in new places.)

MARCH HARE: Stop being so smart. You might learn something.

ALICE: But what happens when you come to the beginning again?

MARCH HARE: Suppose we change the subject. Tell us a story. Who are you?

ALICE: Well, I knew who I was when I got up this morning, but I've changed several times since then.

MAD HATTER: Take some more tea.

ALICE: I haven't had any, so I can't take more.

MAD HATTER: You mean you can't take less. It's very easy to take more than nothing.

MARCH HARE: Wake up, dormouse.

DORMOUSE: I heard every word you fellows were saying.

MARCH HARE: *(To DORMOUSE.)* Tell us the story *(To ALICE.)* Don't *you* want him to tell us a story?

ALICE: I want to play croquet with the queen. And I shall! Oh, why is everything so confusing here?!

DORMOUSE: Once upon a time, there were three little sisters, and they lived at the bottom of a well.

ALICE: How could they live at the bottom of a well? They would drown.

DORMOUSE: It was a treacle-well.

ALICE: What's treacle?

HATTER and HARE: Molasses!

ALICE: There's no such thing as a treacle-well!

HARE AND HATTER: SHHHH!!!!!!!

MARCH HARE: Mind your manners.

DORMOUSE: If you can't be civil, you'd better finish the story yourself.

ALICE: I don't *know* the — *(Stopping herself.)* Carry on.

DORMOUSE: So, these three little sisters were learning to draw… *(He begins to fall asleep.)*

ALICE: What did they draw?

DORMOUSE: Treacle!

ALICE: I don't understand!

MAD HATTER: You can draw water out of a water-well, so I should think you could draw treacle out of a treacle-well, eh, stupid!

ALICE: But if they were *in* the well, how could they —

MARCH HARE: You're thinking again!

(The three burst into laughter.)

ALICE: I've a right to think!

MARCH HARE: Upside down?

ALICE: Why not!

MARCH HARE: Keep your temper.

DORMOUSE: They were learning to draw all manner of things that begin with an "M."

HATTER and HARE: Mmmmmm.

ALICE: Why with an "M?"

MAD HATTER: Why not?

(ALICE is so puzzled that, for once, she has no answer.)

MAD HATTER: What does the flame of a candle look like once it's blown out?

ALICE: I...

DORMOUSE: Mousetraps, the moon, memory, muchness...

MARCH HARE: Ever see a drawing of muchness?

ALICE: I... don't know.

MAD HATTER: Then you shouldn't talk.

(THE MAD HATTER, the MARCH HARE and the DORMOUSE burst into laughter. ALICE, furious, confused, and frightened, jumps up.)

ALICE: Stop it! This is the stupidest tea party I was ever at in all my life. I shall never ever come here again.

(THE DORMOUSE is now asleep in the middle of the table cloth. THE MARCH HARE and the MAD HATTER

begin to drag him off by the corners of the cloth. But suddenly all three freeze.)

ALICE: What's happening?

DORMOUSE: *(Waking up far more sinisterly.)* Who are you? Why are you here?

ALICE: I don't know! I don't know!!! But I do know that I'm Alice! *Alice!* And I'd very much like to go home this instant. I've had quite enough of living upside down!

(The MAD HATTER and MARCH HARE now shift positions and hold up a tiny door. They are neutral now, like stagehands.)

ALICE: Oh, but the door. The garden! *(ALICE crosses slowly to the door.)* I must fit. I must! *(ALICE reaches for the door.)*

End of Scene.

CHAPTER SIX
Scenes for Groups

The Audition From *What Part Will I Play?*

CHARACTERS: (13 w)
> Brittany
> Tiffany
> Erica
> Enid
> Mike
> Zora
> Karina
> Marley
> Jessie
> Amy
> Frances
> Desiree
> Chase
> Stage Manager (Offstage male voice.)

Setting
> An empty stage in a theatre

> What Part Will I Play? *is a play that gives voice to middle school girls' hopes and dreams, fears and failures, fantasies and hard knocks. The girls arrive at a theatre to audition for a promising new play. Each girl has come with her own ambitions, dreams, even secrets. But when the girls learn that the director will be late, they must each wait. As the play progresses, barriers are broken down, friendships and sometimes just tolerances are made, and dreams re-engaged. This is the opening scene.*

(A spotlight hits the back curtain. MUSIC. [Like the song "On Broadway."] One by one, each actor enters through an opening in the upstage curtain. Each assumes a place on the stage, strikes a pose, and remains frozen until all the girls have arrived. Each girl's entrance, reaction to the other girls, and place she assumes reflects who she is and how she feels about this audition.

Once assembled, the girls begin a MOVEMENT PIECE in which they begin to size one another up — seeing who is different, who appears to fit into what group, who might be the stiffest competition for the parts in the play. BRITTANY is featured in a solo moment, showing her skill and confidence as a dancer. TIFFANY and DESIREE circle each other; FRANCES breaks through their circle. The entire group gives MARLEY a look, who through a dance move, tells them to leave her alone. Then the group gives KARINA a look, and she shrinks into the corner. The piece ends in a freeze, which then breaks into the girls, nervously chattering, waiting for the director to arrive.)

STAGE MANAGER: *(A voice-over.)* All right, everyone. Could you line up down stage, please?
(The girls quickly form a line along the downstage edge of the stage, some taking the lead to get to a good place.)
STAGE MANAGER: I'm the stage manager for today's audition.
BRITTANY: *(Stepping forward.)* I'm Brittany Taylor.
FRANCES: *(Stepping forward.)* I'm Frances Elizabeth Phillips…Frances *Louise* Elizabeth Phillips. I —
STAGE MANAGER: Thank you. You'll all have a chance to introduce yourselves in a moment.

FRANCES: I can wait.

STAGE MANAGER: The director will be arriving late this morning.

TIFFANY: You mean, you're not the director?

STAGE MANAGER: No. She's in a meeting with the playwright. As you all know, you're auditioning for a new play today — a play that's scheduled to open in the city next year if everything goes well. But right now, there're still some details to be worked out.

BRITTANY: Like who gets what part.

ENID: How exciting!

(ENID receives a "what a nerd" look from a number of the girls.)

FRANCES: How long do we have to wait?

STAGE MANAGER: Anyone who doesn't want to wait is free to leave now. *(Pause.)* Anyone? *(Pause.)* Fine. Now, I need you to give me your name, and what kind of part you're interested in playing.

MIKE: Excuse me. Do you help with casting?

STAGE MANAGER: Let's just keep this brief and keep it moving. OK? Let's start on this end.

JESSIE: Me?

STAGE MANAGER: Stage right.

(The girls cross center one by one to introduce themselves, then cross to take a place at the other end of the line.)

JESSIE: I'm Jessie Kravitz. I didn't know we were going to have to say this, so I don't know what to say. So I'll say, I don't know. Whatever.

AMY: I'm Amy McKee. I'd be happy to play any part. I just like being in plays.

TIFFANY: Hi. My name is Tiffany. Tiffany Chambers. I usually play somebody important or somebody pretty because, *(Giggles.)* well, I mean, you know.

BRITTANY: Brittany Taylor. You could have checked with my agent, World Class Talent. Since you didn't, check my resume. I always play the lead.

CHASE: I'm Chase Mitchell. I heard you might need a tomboy type. That's me.

DESIREE: That's definitely *not* me. I'm about as much girl as you can get. I'm Desiree Mouduez. I'd like to play the flirtatious friend or the lover — something I'm good at.

MIKE: *(Reacting to Desiree.)* Ooooo, boy! Well, Mike's the name. It's my nickname, but you can call me Mike, all the same. Hey, I'm a poet and didn't know it. Did I show it? *(She waits for a laugh. Nothing.)* If you need a comedian, you've found her. Right here on your very own stage. It's your lucky day.

ENID: My name is Enid Buttersworth. I'd like to play the heroine.

ERICA: I'm Erica Downing. I'd like *(Looking around her.)* a normal part.

ZORA: I'm Zora. I have the energy inside myself to make any part my own. I am completely open.

FRANCES: Finally! I'm Frances Louise Elizabeth Phillips. I've been in so many plays that it's hard to remember what parts I like best. I'm really good at everything, but especially a part with lots of lines.

KARINA: I think I'm different from everybody here. I don't know if you'll have a part to fit me. Oh. I'm Karina...James.

MARLEY: *(Big pause.)* I'm Marley. You figure it out.

STAGE MANAGER: Thank you. Now, divide into groups of three, please. You'll be doing some improvisations for the director when she arrives.

TIFFANY: You mean we have to be in a group, with like, other people?

DESIREE: Do you get to be in a group, sir?

MIKE: Boy, that would be funny. But I think everything is

funny. I'm really very funny myself. In fact… Hello? Are you there? *(The STAGE MANAGER has left them alone.)*

MIKE: Mr. Stage Manager?

MARLEY: Think he's tuned you out, funny one.

MIKE: Oh. Well. That's OK. So who wants to be in my group? *(MIKE raises her hand. No one responds. There is an awkward pause among the group about everything.)*

MIKE: Anybody?

ERICA: I don't understand what's going on. Why isn't the director here?

BRITTANY: They're just trying to shake us up. That's what an audition is all about. Seeing who can take it. *(Some girls now move uncomfortably out of the line.)*

ENID: I think it's been great fun so far.

FRANCES: You would.

AMY: I think we should just do what he says. The director will get here soon. So here's one group. *(She raises her hand.)*

BRITTANY: Here's another. *(Raising her hand.)*

MARLEY: Great. Now we can choose between Goldilocks and the movie star.

ENID: That's not very nice.

TIFFANY: When's a stoner ever been nice. *(Pause, as MARLEY and TIFFANY face off.)*

JESSIE: *(To MARLEY.)* I'll be in your group.

MARLEY: I don't need a group.

DESIREE: Does anybody get the point of this? If we knew what the director wanted, we'd know how to divide up.

ENID: What do you mean?

TIFFANY: Like, you know.

ENID: Know what?

FRANCES: Ga, you are really a geek, aren't you.

ENID: Actually, a bookie is what I am usually called.

MIKE: You ought to hear what I'm usually called. I'm…

FRANCES: Save it, Mike.

MIKE: Sure. I'll save it. No problem.

DESIREE: I mean, does (*Calling up to the booth.*) this probably extremely good-looking stage manager want all the preppies together?

MARLEY: What a new and exciting idea.

DESIREE: Who asked you.

AMY: I really don't think the groups matter.

CHASE: OK. Who wants to be with the jock? You'll get a great chance at the girlie parts if she compares you to me.

DESIREE: Great idea. (*Moves toward CHASE.*)

TIFFANY: Desiree. (*DESIREE stops.*) Really.

ERICA: (*To TIFFANY and DESIREE.*) I'll be in your group.

TIFFANY: I guess that's OK.

FRANCES: Another wanna-be preppie achieves success.

DESIREE: Jealous?

FRANCES: Are you kidding? I've got millions of friends. I get invited to a party every weekend. I'm on the phone every night for three hours.

ZORA: You know, I never find talking on the phone to be as meaningful as one-to-one communication.
(*No one really has a comeback.*)

ENID: (*To ZORA.*) I'll be in your group.

ZORA: Cool.

BRITTANY: Look guys, just get with the person who'll make you look the best. This is a competition. There're not enough parts for all of us. There never are.

STAGE MANAGER: OK, girls. Divide.
(*The girls move self-consciously into groups of three. TIFFANY, DESIREE, and ERICA join up; ENID, ZORA, and KARINA join; MIKE, CHASE, and FRANCES join; JESSIE, AMY, and BRITTANY join. MARLEY is left out.*)

MUSIC [pulsing rock] begins. A spotlight hits MARLEY. The other girls freeze.)

MARLEY: Big surprise who gets left out, huh. I'm used to this. I *want* it. I don't want to be like the rest of these people. A clone, skipping along the path that everybody follows. Who needs it. Nobody here can understand me. Nobody even wants to try to understand that maybe I dress different because I feel different. I feel angry. 'Cause I don't know if I'll ever get a part — anywhere.

End of Scene.

To Fly

Adapted from "The Woman Who Fell from the Sky," in
Walking the Winds: American Tales.

CHARACTERS: (11 actors: 5 m, 6 w)
    (All are ages 11–13)
    Gloria (w)
    Kendra (w)
    Nora (w)
    Keanu (m)
    Michael (m)
    Inez (w)
    Mia (w)
    Adam (m)
    Daren (m)
    Rasheed (m)
    Jewel (w)

SETTING:
    A middle school classroom

*Eleven middle schoolers have a class assignment to
create a play based on an Iroquois creation story. As the
scene begins, GLORIA and KENDRA are attempting to
determine the best way to carry NORA. KEANU,
MICHAEL, INEZ, and MIA are coaching. ADAM, shy and
small, is sitting off to the side, with his nose buried in a
book.*

INEZ: Can we at least try my idea? Nora can stand on your shoulders.

MIA: Great! Like in cheerleading.

KENDRA: Then she'll look like she's really flying. Here, I'll get down on one knee — *(She does.)*

NORA: I don't know about this.

INEZ: It'll work!

NORA: How do I get up there?

MICHAEL: You take gymnastics. Do a flip or something.

NORA, KENDRA, and GLORIA: Very funny.

KEANU: He's just trying to be helpful.

INEZ: If you really want to help, lift her up there.

MIA: Yeah!

NORA: Oh no. I'll get up myself.

MICHAEL: Come on, Nora. You couldn't weigh *that* much.

KEANU: How much pizza did you have for lunch?

MIA: You guys!

ADAM: *(Looking up from his book.)* She had yogurt and carrots. Three carrots.

(Everyone flashes him a look.)

ADAM: I just happened to notice.

GLORIA: You *notice* what she eats?

ADAM: I notice a lot.

INEZ: You're so weird.

(ADAM looks back into his book.)

NORA: Look, I'll step up on a chair first.

GLORIA: No props or furniture, remember? We've got to do this whole play just with our voices and our bodies.

MIA: That was the assignment.

MICHAEL: But we gotta have special effects. Let's get her, Keanu.

(MICHAEL and KEANU pick up NORA, despite her protests. They try to put her on the shoulders of GLORIA and KENDRA.)

NORA: Hey! What are you...Careful!

(The group ad-libs warnings and instructions to the boys, until finally they all topple to the ground. They are laughing, all except for NORA.)

NORA: I don't think this is funny. I'm the one who is going to look stupid in front of the whole school.

INEZ: Maybe you guys can be the loons. Boys can be loons, too.

GLORIA: *That's* for sure.

MICHAEL: Loony-tunes!

KENDRA: Let's switch parts, Keanu. Who were you?

KEANU: The snapping turtle. I don't know if you can handle that part.

MIA: We *all* wrote the script.

GLORIA: So we can all play any part. Kendra and I will split up.

(DAREN, RASHEED, and JEWEL enter.)

DAREN: Hold up, everybody. Did I just hear Gloria suggest that she and Kendra split up? You mean, they are actually not gonna be next to each other at all times? Will they survive??

GLORIA: Grow up, Daren.

KEANU: Anyone who's late for practice should keep their comments to themselves.

RASHEED: I've been havin' more fun outside the door, watchin' you guys look stupid.

JEWEL: Nora, you really *are* gonna be the woman who falls from the sky if that's how you let them carry you.

INEZ: We worked out a way to do it in drama class. We were just experimenting with another idea.

MIA: That's legal.

JEWEL: Why mess it up? We've practiced it already.

DAREN: OK. OK. Now that the important people are here, let the show begin!

(Some of the students begin to move into place.)

NORA: I think I liked falling from the sky the old way, Inez. Is that OK?

INEZ: Sure, I was just exercising my imagination.

MICHAEL: And made us bust our muscles. *(Dramatically.)* Ahh, my back!

NORA: I weigh a ton, don't I.

KENDRA: Here we go again.

NORA: Maybe I shouldn't play this part. Maybe I'm too fat.

JEWEL: You're not too fat. You are perfect. Now let's do this. It counts for half our grade, remember?

DAREN: Places everybody.

(The students move into their opening positions, ad-libbing expressions of their excitement. RASHEED stands on the sidelines.)

KEANU: Rasheed, "Places" means "Get ready." What're you doin'?

RASHEED: If you guys really think I'm gonna play a muskrat, then you are wrong, wrong, wrong.

MIA: But we all voted. That's the part you got.

GLORIA: Adam counted the ballots, right?

ADAM: Huh?

INEZ: The ballots. You counted them.

ADAM: Absolutely. Very accurately.

RASHEED: Did you, Math-man? Well, I didn't vote.

MICHAEL: That was your choice. This is a democracy.

INEZ: And in a democracy you have to exercise your right to vote.

JEWEL: What, is this a project for government class now? Get over it, Rasheed, or fail literature class.

KEANU: Look, Rasheed, just play the muskrat. He's the hero.

ADAM: I'll do it.

(A beat of silence as everyone looks at ADAM in amazement.)

RASHEED: That's a joke.

KENDRA: Why not? You don't want to do it.

RASHEED: But I don't want him to do it.

GLORIA: In this group we only offer constructive criticism!

RASHEED: Then construct yourself taller, Adam. You're a shrimp.

MIA: Rasheed!

GLORIA: Look, we all worked on this script together, we all came up with the ideas, and we all decided who would play what.

JEWEL: And it is too late to change everything now.

RASHEED: Here's one thing that's changin'. I'm outta here.

KENDRA: You can't quit. We're a group!

MICHAEL: And it'll screw up our grade.

INEZ: Isn't there some part you wanna do?

RASHEED: I'll do it, if I can be a bird — one of the loons.

GLORIA: He just wants to get his hands on Nora!

MICHAEL: We're the loons, man. Take a number.

JEWEL: What's the big deal? Would somebody just switch!

KEANU: Give me one good reason why I should switch, Rasheed.

RASHEED: I wanna... Forget it.

KEANU: Come on. One good reason.

(Everyone waits for an answer. RASHEED is defensive, but honest in his reply.)

RASHEED: I wanna fly. Feel what it's like. That OK with you?

KEANU: Sure, man. It's all yours.

NORA: On one condition.

MICHAEL: What?

NORA: Adam gets to play the muskrat.

ADAM: You want me to, Nora? Really?

NORA: You'll be great.

DAREN: Step up to the plate, Muskrat-man.

JEWEL: Let's do it.

(The students are now ready. They are very committed to their roles now, and they are very inventive with their voices and bodies as they create all of the images and characters as the story unfolds. Directors may want to underscore the story with music.)

ALL: In the beginning.

RASHEED, DAREN, KENDRA, MIA, ADAM: There was only water.

KEANU, MICHAEL, GLORIA, INEZ, JEWEL: And the animals who lived in it.

KENDRA, MIA: All was at peace.

RASHEED, MICHAEL: But then —

RASHEED, DAREN, KENDRA, MIA, ADAM: A great wind blew from the heavens.

KEANU, MICHAEL, GLORIA, INEZ, JEWEL: And swept across the water.

KENDRA, MIA, GLORIA: Then a woman —

ALL FEMALE VOICES: A woman whose body was shining.

ALL: As if it was the sun.

NORA: A woman fell from a torn place in the sky.

ALL FEMALE VOICES: A divine woman. Full of power.

RASHEED, MICHAEL: Two loons saw her and flew under her.

KENDRA, MIA: Making a pillow for her to sit on.

RASHEED, MICHAEL: They cried for help.

GLORIA, INEZ, JEWEL, DAREN, KEANU, KENDRA, MIA: The animals heard their cries. And came.

RASHEED, MICHAEL: The loons put her on the great snapping turtle's back.

GLORIA: You may have my back as your home.

INEZ: But the duck replied, "No. There must be earth where she can stand."

JEWEL: The seal said, "I will dive to the ocean's bottom and find the earth."

DAREN: But the otter thought this was impossible. "Who can swim so deep?"

INEZ: The duck dove beneath the water —

KEANU: And the beaver swam swiftly down —

GLORIA, JEWEL, DAREN: But they could not reach the bottom.

MICHAEL: A loon shot like an arrow into the darkness of the sea.

RASHEED: But he, too, could not reach bottom.

ADAM: I will try.

GLORIA, INEZ, JEWEL, DAREN, KEANU, KENDRA, MIA: The muskrat!

GLORIA: So small!

RASHEED: So slow!

INEZ, JEWEL, DAREN: He swam down and down —

JEWEL: Until his lungs almost burst. But once his tiny paw touched the bottom —

MUSKRAT: He clutched a tiny speck of earth then sped up and up until he burst back up into the light!

KENDRA and MIA: The swans lifted the woman between their wings.

GLORIA, INEZ, JEWEL, DAREN, KEANU, KENDRA, MIA: And the sea animals placed the tiny speck of earth on the turtle's back.

KENDRA and MIA: As they spread it around and around it became larger —

GLORIA, INEZ, JEWEL, DAREN, KEANU: And larger—

GLORIA, INEZ, JEWEL, DAREN, KEANU, KENDRA, MIA: Until it became the whole world.

RASHEED: The woman walked gently onto the new earth.

KENDRA: And dropped a handful of seeds —

NORA: Seeds that I bring from the sky world. Seeds from a

great tree, with roots growing to the east, south, west and
north. From these seeds life on this new earth will begin.

ADAM: What will it be like?

JEWEL: What will grow?

DAREN: Who will live here?

NORA: From the seeds I have planted, all things will grow.
Plants the color of turtle's back.
Flowers as bright as the muskrat's eyes.
Trees that soar as high as the loons at sunset.

MICHAEL: Will there be animals who crawl and hop and
run?

RASHEED: And men who walk and dream?

KENDRA: And women and children —

JEWEL: Who will have children, and children, and children
again?

NORA: Yes. On this new earth, all things will grow for always.
*(They make a final tableau. Then they burst out of it,
with a big shout.)*

ALL: All right!

INEZ: That was the best we've ever done it!

GLORIA: You flew great, Nora.

NORA: So did you, Rasheed.

RASHEED: Yeah.
(ADAM has returned to his corner to read his book.)

MICHAEL: Let's fly somebody else. Come here.
*(MICHAEL huddles for a second with KEANU, DAREN,
and JEWEL. The others watch, ad-lib whispers of
"What's up?" Then MICHAEL, KEANU, DAREN and
JEWEL sweep up behind ADAM and lift him up on their
shoulders.)*

ADAM: Hey, wait. I don't fly in this play.

NORA: But you made the world. And saved the play.

ALL: *(Ad-libbing.)* Yeah, Adam. / Way to go, Muskrat. / *(And
so forth.)*

ADAM: Thanks.

JEWEL: Let's go. The bell's gonna ring for second period. We've gotta get set up for the show.

(The students all grab book bags, etc., and exit hurriedly out of the classroom. NORA waits for ADAM, and walks with him. RASHEED is last to leave. He turns back into the now empty performance space. He lifts his arms in a pose of a flying bird — trying on the freedom once again. Then exits.)

End of Scene.

Parents   Adapted from *What Part Will I Play?*

CHARACTERS: (Min. 5 w, or 4 w/1m. Can be 11 actors or more.)

    Frances

    Meg

    Tiffany

    *Mom (can be played by 1–4 or more actors.)

    *Dad (can be played by 1–4 or more actors.)

SETTING:

    An empty stage in a theatre

In this fantasy scene, three young women each shares her image of her parents. Ideally, several actors create the two larger-than-life parents (perhaps miming a man's suit, brief case, and hat for Dad, and a woman's sweat suit, visor, and tennis racket for Mom.) The parents' voices should be created by several actors speaking together. Music can be used to underscore the scene. [This scene is from an all-female cast play, but it is equally powerful when performed with young men creating the Dad.]

(FRANCES, MEG, and TIFFANY are each in their own space, facing down stage. They are talking directly to the audience.)

FRANCES: I know I'm not the only kid ever to have problems with her parents, but my problems —

MEG: My problems—

TIFFANY: What problems?

FRANCES: Are mine!

MEG: Are different!

MEG, TIFFANY, and FRANCES: Parents!

MEG: Why don't you try to really understand me?

ALL ACTORS: Parents!!

FRANCES: I wish I could tell you how I really feel.

ALL ACTORS: Parents!!!

(The huge MOM and DAD are created by the actors. TIFFANY skips out to talk to them.)

TIFFANY: Hi, Mom.

MOM: *(Several voices.)* Hello, dear.

TIFFANY: Hi, Dad.

DAD: *(Several voices.)* Hello, dear.

TIFFANY: I'm home from school.

MOM and DAD: That's wonderful, dear.

TIFFANY: Listen.

MOM and DAD: We're listening.

TIFFANY: Can I go over to my friend's house after school on Friday? She's having a swimming party.

MOM: Why of course, dear.

DAD: Anything you like, dear.

TIFFANY: Gee, thanks, Mom and Dad. You're terrific.

MOM and DAD: We know, dear.

TIFFANY: An example of the perfect parents, as conceived by the middle school child. *(She skips offstage.)*

MEG: The following is an example somewhat closer to reality. Hi, Mom.

MOM: Hello, dear.

MEG: Hi, Dad. *(No reply.)* Hi, Dad!

DAD: Oh, hello, dear.

MEG: May I go over to my friend's house after school on Friday? She's having a swimming party.

MOM: Will there be a lifeguard?

MEG: What?

DAD: Will there be any *boys* there?

MEG: Hope so.

MOM: Who's driving?

DAD: Any drinking?

MEG: Just Cokes.

MOM: How many?

DAD: What ages?

MEG: *(Joking.)* The Cokes?

MOM and DAD: Don't use that tone of voice with *us*, young
    lady.

MEG: What voice? What tone? What did I say?

MOM: That's enough!

DAD: You're grounded.

MOM: For a month. No TV.

DAD: No phone.

MOM: No computer.

DAD: Absolutely no fun—

MOM and DAD: Until you're 21!!

MEG: But, Dad!

MOM and DAD: Meg!!!

MEG: Now that's reality.

FRANCES: Wanna see what it's like at my house? Try this.
    Hi, Mom and Dad. I'm home.

    (The PARENTS are now distracted, slightly turned away.)

MOM: Fine, dear.

FRANCES: I got all A's on my report card.

DAD: Fine, dear.

FRANCES: Do you want to see it?

MOM: Fine, dear.

FRANCES: My teacher asked me to stay after class so she
    could tell me how well I was doing.

DAD: Fine, dear.

FRANCES: Then she took me out for an ice cream.

MOM: Fine, dear.

FRANCES: I had eleven scoops.

DAD: Hummm…

FRANCES: Then we drove to Mexico.

MOM: Humm…

FRANCES: Then I flew to the moon!!

DAD: Humm…

FRANCES: Are you listening?

MOM: Frances, your Father and I are having a little party on Friday night. Do you think you could go visit a friend or something?

FRANCES: You don't want me here?

DAD: Some friends from the office, Frances. It's an important party for us, dear.

FRANCES: So you want me out of the way?

MOM: Just this once, dear.

FRANCES: You always say that. Are you that embarrassed by me? Is everything more important to you than me?
(The PARENTS turn their backs on FRANCES.)

FRANCES: No! Pay attention to me! Please…
(The PARENTS begin to disappear.)

FRANCES: Then forget it. I don't care about you either. No… Mom…please!

ALL ACTORS: Don't bother us, Frances. Stay out of the way, Frances. Don't bother us, Frances. Stay out of the way, Frances.

FRANCES: *(Overlapping.)* Stop it!

MEG: *(Overlapping.)* Mom! Dad!

ALL ACTORS: *(Overlapping.)* Yes, No, Yes, No, Yes, No…

TIFFANY: *(Overlapping.)* Mom?

ALL ACTORS: *(Whispering, fading.)* Parents!
(The PARENTS have disappeared. The girls are left alone on stage. The fantasy ends.)

End of Scene.

The Promise
Adapted from *La Mascarada de la Vida*

CHARACTERS: (8 actors: 2 m, 2 w, *4 m and/or w)
Paz (m)
Dona Sebastiana (w)
Leonor (w)
Marina*
Emillo*
Juanita*
Jose*
Commacho (m)

SETTING:
Outside of a poor Mexican Village, then in the Village square.

In my play La Mascarada de la Vida, *PAZ is a poor peasant in Mexico who struggles to build a life for himself with LEONOR. COMMACHO, the unjust mayor of PAZ's village, forces PAZ to travel to the next village to sell his chickens. On his journey, PAZ meets DONA SEBASTIANA (Death or La Muerta in Mexican folklore). He shares one of his chickens with her, and in return he is given the power to heal — to be a* curandero.

(DONA SEBASTIANA, an elegant feminine character, has just handed PAZ a small pouch made of sackcloth on a leather necklace.)
PAZ: Dona Sebastiana, I thought you would come to take my life, not my just my chicken.

DONA SEBASTIANA: *(Laughing.)* Today, Paz, I was hungry only for food. And as thanks, I give you this.

PAZ: *(A little frightened.)* What is it?

DONA SEBASTIANA: When you place this pouch around your neck, you will have a special power — a power from the earth, from the sea and sky. You will be a curandero!

PAZ: A curandero! A healer? Me?

DONA SEBASTIANA: Si.

PAZ: You mean, if I am sick, I can make myself well again?

DONA SEBASTIANA: You can make anyone well again, if that is what you desire. But, you must use your power well.

PAZ: I will!

DONA SEBASTIANA: And you must promise one thing. If you are called to heal someone, and you see me standing at the head of the bed, you must not heal that person. Their time has come. But, if I am standing at the foot of the bed, then you may use your power.

PAZ: That is a simple promise to keep. Gracias, Dona Sebastiana, Gracias.

DONA SEBASTIANA: *(Exiting slowly, but calling back.)* Remember your promise and use your gift well.

PAZ: I have met *La Muerta!* Death!! *(He puts the small pouch, which DONA SEBASTIANA has given him, around his neck.)* I will use my gift well, Dona Sebastiana. Leonor! I must tell Leonor!

(PAZ begins his journey back to his village. He is quickly met upon the road by MARINA, a peasant.)

MARINA: Senor Curandero? Senor?

PAZ: Me? Yes, that is me!

MARINA: My father, he has a terrible fever. His body is like fire. Please, you must help me!

PAZ: *(Clasping the pouch.)* Make a warm tea to drink from the tiny flowers and leaves of the borraja plant.

MARINA: The borraja. Si.

PAZ: Once he sips the tea three times at each hour of the clock for one day —

MARINA: Three time, each hour, one day.

PAZ: The fire in his body will turn to ash and his fever will disappear.

MARINA: *(Exiting.)* Oh gracias, senor. Gracias!

PAZ: I did very well, si? That is, if it works!

EMILLO: *(Entering.)* Senor! My ankle.

PAZ: Another?

EMILLO: It hurts to walk. It hurts to move. It hurts to say how it hurts to move.

PAZ: Your ankle is crying for rest. Give it a bath with the warm oil from the olive, then put it to bed for three days.

EMILLO: Three days??

PAZ: No more, no less. Ah, think of the warm oil, right at the joint!

EMILLO: *(Exiting.)* Ooo. Just the thought makes my ankle sing with joy. Gracias.

PAZ: De nada, my friend.

JUANITA: *(Entering.)* Senor! My baby! He will not stop crying, and fussing, and crying and —

PAZ: He cries because he is cold in his stomach. A warm herb will bring balance to his tiny body. Give him a rich tea of manzanilla.

JUANITA: Manzanilla, manzanilla, manzanilla —

PAZ: And light two candles, candles as blue as the summer sky, to bring tranquillity to your house.

JUANITA: *(Exiting.)* Blue candles, manzanilla, manzanilla, blue candles —

PAZ: She looks like she could use some tranquillity.

JOSE: *(Entering, staggering.)* Auooo! There is a war in my stomach!

PAZ: Too much fiesta?

JOSE: Si.

PAZ: To stop the battle, drink a tea of yerba buena. This will chase all those devils away.

JOSE: Gracias, my friend. I will remember — *(Getting sick.)* your kindness. *(He exits quickly.)*

PAZ: Si, si! Hurry! Four sicknesses, and I have given four cures. But wait! This might be a dream! Tomorrow I could wake, and find myself a chicken seller once again. Or...could the heavens be smiling on me? Could —
(Each PEASANT circles back through quickly and bestows a gift upon PAZ. They gather around him.)

MARINA: My father's fever, it is gone. Por favor, I give you the finest vegetables from my garden as thanks.

PAZ: What?

EMILLO: Senor curandero! My ankle! It has healed! I can walk! I can dance!! Gracias! *(Hands him another basket of food.)* Gracias!

JUANITA: My baby. He is a much better now. *(Hands him a bunch of flowers.)* Gracias senor, curandero.

PAZ: "Curandero?!"

JOSE: My stomach — good as new. *(Hands him a bottle of drink and winks.)* See you at the next fiesta, si?

PAZ: It is true! I *am* a curandero.
(PAZ is laughing with joyous delight, his arms filled with the presents from the PEASANTS when LEONOR enters.)

LEONOR: Paz? Paz! I have been searching and searching for you. I have been so worried!

PAZ: You will never worry again, Leonor. Today, we begin a new life!

LEONOR: What? Where did you get all of these things? Our three chickens could not sell for so much that you could buy all of this!

MARINA: They are presents!

EMILLO: Of thanks!

LEONOR: Thanks? For what? *(Pulling PAZ away from the group.)* Paz, you did not steal —

PAZ: I would never steal!

JOSE: He is Paz, the curandero!

JUANITA: He has brought health to each of us.

EMILLO: To all of us!

LEONOR: Paz, I think the hot sun is making you and your friends say strange thoughts. Sit down for a moment. Take a rest -—

PAZ: We say only what is true! I have been given a great gift. The gift of the curandero.

LEONOR: Who could give you such a gift?

PAZ: A...friend.

(Enter COMMACHO with big whooping cough. It is uncontrollable. He is in great need of healing.)

PAZ: Ha! Since you think that the sun has made me loco, I will show you my new power. And on someone I would like very much to "make better!"

JOSE: Commacho, the mayor!

LEONOR: You mustn't anger Commacho with your foolishness! He will only change the laws again to harm us even more.

PAZ: You will see. *(To COMMACHO.)* Buenos tardes, Senor Commacho.

COMMACHO: *(Coughing.)* Out of my way! All of you. Can't you see I am ill. *(Coughing again. The PEASANTS are frightened of him, and move away, but they remain to watch. LEONOR tries to draw PAZ back to the PEASANTS.)*

LEONOR: Paz!

PAZ: Yes, I see, Senor. That is why you must sit down, so I can help you.

COMMACHO: You, help *me!* *(Cough.)*

PAZ: I have the power to make you well again. But first you must sit.

COMMACHO: Well, I am desperate. All right, peasant. But if you fail!!!

PAZ: Sit, sit. First, I must put this leaf around your neck. The sweet smell is soothing, si? *(COMMACHO grunts.)* Now, this powder of bark and root, to encircle you with the power of the earth. And this water on your forehead to cool you.

(DONA SEBASTIANA enters, visible only to PAZ. She looks at COMMACHO and ponders for a moment)

DONA SEBASTIANA: Mmmmm. Not yet.

(She crosses and stands at COMMACHO's feet. She and PAZ exchange a wink and PAZ continues.)

PAZ: Now, Senor Commacho. You have this sickness because an evil wind has brought it into your body. Now this evil wind chose your body for a reason. What have you done wrong lately?

COMMACHO: Wrong? Me? Nothing. *(A great cough.)*

PAZ: Think again, senor. Surely some little something. Have you argued with your wife lately?

COMMACHO: No.

PAZ: Have you offended any of your friends? Not invited them to a fiesta?

COMMACHO: Of course not!

PAZ: Have you made any laws lately that are not fair?

COMMACHO: Never! *(Huge cough.)*

EMILLO: *(Getting braver.)* Never?

COMMACHO: Well...I did change the laws for the marketplace. *Perhaps* they are not fair. *(Coughs.)* Yes, yes, they are not fair. All right! I will change them back, so that everyone can sell their wares where they like. *(His cough disappears.)* My cough! It is gone. Senor Paz, you are a fine curandero. My thanks.

PAZ: De nada!

COMMACHO: And here. *(Tosses him a bag of money, and exits.)*

LEONOR: Paz! You *do* have a great gift.

JUANITA: And look how much he paid you for it!

LEONOR: I have never seen such money.

PAZ: Each coin, each tiny wonderful coin is —

LEONOR: Paz! We must use it wisely.

> *(They both dutifully nod, and then burst into delighted laughter, and toss the money bag in the air. The PEASANTS share in their laughter and celebration.)*

LEONOR: To think that your gift can be used for such good!

PAZ: Today, our new life begins!

DONA SEBASTIANA: *(Stepping into the celebration, heard only by PAZ.)* Remember your promise!

PAZ: I do! I will! Gracias, La Muerta.

DONA SEBASTIANA: Remember!

End of Scene.

Ghost Train

Adapted from "The Iron Moonhunter," in *Walking the Winds: American Tales.*

CHARACTERS: (Min. 9 actors. Can be up to 15–20. Any combination of m or w. Historically, all characters would be male.)

Chinese Storyteller
Kwan Ming, the youngest brother
Kwan Cheong, the middle brother
Kwan Hop, the oldest brother
American Storyteller
Railway Foreman
Ah Ding, the cook
Wong, a worker
Jeong Yum, a worker
*Other workers
*Ghosts
(* Also part of the ensemble that creates, along with all the characters, the effects of the play.)

SETTING:

Various locales

This short play is based on the legend of the Iron Moonhunter, a ghost train said to be built by the Chinese who came to America in the nineteenth century to build the railroads. This is an ensemble piece with many different parts. Its power comes not in trying to realistically create the setting and sequences, but in using actors and their bodies, and long wooden poles to create all environments and effects. The poles can define space, suggest railroad ties, and be knocked against the floor to create the rhythm of driving spikes. The one scenic element you may wish to realize is the dragon-train itself. (In the original production, it was a huge Chinese Dragon puppet, whose face resembled the front grid of a steam locomotive.) This piece provides an exciting challenge, especially for young male actors.

As the scene begins, the ENSEMBLE creates a boat crossing the Pacific Ocean to America.

CHINESE STORYTELLER: Once there were three brothers from China. One day they boarded a huge ship to sail to Gum Hahn — The Golden Mountain. This was the name the Chinese gave to America.
   (The ENSEMBLE of actors create a boat and its passengers. The KWAN BROTHERS stand together, looking out over the water.)

KWAN MING: *(To his older brothers.)* Will we see silver glistening on the hillsides? And gold shining from the bottom of shallow springs? And —

KWAN CHEONG: Soon we will have our own house —

KWAN MING: Our own horse and cart!

KWAN HOP: But we must promise to be forever brothers in this land which is not our home. We must take care of one another. Always.

KWAN MING: Look! Across the water.

KWAN CHEONG: Where?

KWAN MING: Raising his head! His eyes shining!! *(Nothing is there.)* It is gone.

KWAN CHEONG: If it ever was there.

KWAN MING: I saw it!

KWAN HOP: Perhaps it was the dragon of the sea, sailing beside us. Guarding us on our way.

KWAN MING: Will the dragon follow us to America?

KWAN HOP: I hope so. We will need the dragon's goodness and strength.

CHINESE STORYTELLER: Soon the brothers arrived —
(The boat transforms into the WORKERS gathering, meeting, being given their poles.)

AMERICAN STORYTELLER: In America. They traveled with lots of other Tong Yun — Chinese workers — to the Sierra Nevadas, a mountain range with cavernous valleys and sheer cliffs.

CHINESE STORYTELLER: An impossible place to build a railroad!
(The WORKERS have now assembled in front of their FOREMAN.)

FOREMAN: OK, China boys. We've got ravines to fill, tunnels to dig, and a cliff the size of Texas that's gotta be blasted out. You — *(Pointing to the KWAN BROTHERS.)* Take your team and start levelin' out that railbed. Go on!
(The KWAN BROTHERS and other WORKERS work alongside one another on the railroad. They create rhythmic sounds with the long poles.)

KWAN CHEONG: Why must we do only this job? We are as strong as the others.

KWAN MING: "Little monkeys. Only good for hauling dirt!"

KWAN HOP: Soon they will see what we can do.

KWAN CHEONG: What are you planning?

AH DING: *(Entering.)* Tea! Hot tea in the barrel!

KWAN CHEONG: Why must you set out our teacups? Don't you see it only gives them another thing to taunt us with?

AH DING: I am the cook for this team. And this team drinks tea. Good riddance to them, I say.

KWAN HOP: We must earn their respect.

KWAN MING: How?

KWAN HOP: In China we have built roads on the sides of

great mountains for hundreds of years. We know ways that they do not know.

WONG: From our ancestors.

AH DING: I say let's keep our secrets to ourselves.

KWAN HOP: We must build baskets and hang in them from great ropes. We can swing toward the cliff, place large sticks of dynamite, then swing away with all our might. We will show them how "monkeys" can build a railroad.

CHINESE STORYTELLER: At first the foreman was skeptical.

FOREMAN: Are you crazy?

(The ENSEMBLE creates KWAN HOP in the basket, blasting the hill-side with dynamite.)

AMERICAN STORYTELLER: But the first time Kwan Hop exploded a huge great hole in that cliff, the foreman changed his mind. Soon Kwan Hop and his team were blasting bigger and bigger chunks from the mountain.

(The ENSEMBLE creates illusion of KWAN MING and KWAN HOP swinging slowly in the air together in the basket.)

CHINESE STORYTELLER: Kwan Ming loved to ride with his older brother in the basket. For the few moments that they swung in the air, they felt free.

KWAN HOP: Look with an eagle's eyes, little brother.

KWAN MING: I see a ridge of mountain. Over there. It curves like a dragon's back. He *did* come with us. Do you see?

(The ENSEMBLE shifts, leaving KWAN HOP alone in the basket.)

CHINESE STORYTELLER: But one day, Kwan Hop went up alone in his basket.

AMERICAN STORYTELLER: He was placin' a huge charge of dynamite. He wanted to swing outta there in a hurry.

ALL ACTORS: The blast shook the earth!

CHINESE STORYTELLER: The flash lit the sky like fire. But when Kwan Ming looked up proudly for his brother —
(The ENSEMBLE shifts and the basket disappears.)

KWAN MING: Kwan Hop! The ropes! His basket. He has fallen!

AH DING: I am sorry, Kwan Ming.

KWAN MING: My brother!

AH DING: We must go on.

KWAN MING: But I cannot leave this place. How will he rest, if there is no one here to mourn him?

AH DING: Many have died. Many more will die.

KWAN MING: But —

WONG: We must pray that Kwan Hop will find his rest. There is nothing more we can do.
(The WORKERS begin again their rhythmic work with the poles, which grows slower and slower as they struggle against the winter.)

AMERICAN STORYTELLER: The railroad crew moved on, workin' deeper and deeper into the Sierra Nevadas.

CHINESE STORYTELLER: But soon the cold, terrible winter began, with snow drifts so high that they covered the tops of the towering redwood trees. To survive, the Tong Yun dug caves in the snow and huddled together in thin cotton clothes, waiting for the nights to pass.
(The ENSEMBLE creates the cave.)

KWAN MING: *(Entering.)* Are you here, brother?

KWAN CHEONG: Yes.

KWAN MING: I thought I had lost you. I followed what I thought was the right tunnel in the snow, but it led nowhere!

KWAN CHEONG: You are safe. Rest awhile.

KWAN MING: I saw something today.

KWAN CHEONG: Another of your monsters? You should have left your fantasies in China.

KWAN MING: Not a monster. But...a shadow. I am sure it was Kwan Hop.

KWAN CHEONG: Our brother is dead.

KWAN MING: But I am sure!

KWAN CHEONG: You are only wishing. Wishes die on the Golden Mountain. I have saved the last pieces of a fox that we can eat. Stay here. I will bring it.

KWAN MING: Kwan Cheong, do not leave —

KWAN CHEONG: I will return.

CHINESE STORYTELLER: As Kwan Ming waited, the wind whistled through the tunnels of snow, and the ice creaked and cracked. He felt shivers of fear in his body as well as a numbing, deadly cold.

(A single, plaintive eerie flute is heard, perhaps played by an ENSEMBLE member. And the ghost of KWAN HOP appears at a distance from KWAN MING.)

KWAN MING: Kwan Hop? Brother! *(The ghost looks at him, but does not speak.)* Why do you look at me so? Perhaps I am dreaming.

(Now the ghost of KWAN CHEONG joins the ghost of KWAN HOP and appears at a distance from KWAN MING.)

KWAN MING: Kwan Cheong, do you see? I told you our brother was there. Do you see him? Kwan Hop!

(The ghosts are joined by the ghosts of other WORKERS. They each reach out, as if lost. With AH DING'S entrance, they disappear.)

AH DING: *(Entering with WONG and JEONG YUM.)* Kwan Ming? Are you there? Wake up!

KWAN MING: I am here. You do not speak. What is it?

AH DING: One of the tunnels in the snow has just collapsed. Four men have been buried alive. Kwan Cheong is among them.

KWAN MING: No. He was just here. With Kwan Hop. And with others. I —

AH DING: You were dreaming —

WONG: Was he?

KWAN MING: They were here!

AH DING: They are dead.

WONG: I have seen *my* brother. My brother who is dead. I have seen him, night after night.

JEONG YUM: And my cousin. Killed in the landslide. He follows me. Asking me why he cannot go home.

WONG: Ghost spirits.

JEONG YUM: We are haunted!

AH DING: If our dead cannot rest, it is because of this railroad! Turn our dynamite to it, I say. Destroy it before it destroys us.

KWAN MING: No. For our brothers' sake, we must be proud of our work.

JEONG YUM: But as long as the lost spirits of our brothers walk these mountains, we will know no peace ourselves.

KWAN MING: Then we must bring them peace. We will build our own railroad.

AH DING: We cannot.

KWAN MING: We will build it from the scraps of the white demon's railroad. Scraps from their train wrecks —

JEONG YUM: Yes! From rails they have broken and thrown away.

KWAN MING: We will ride our train to find our brothers and bring them home.

(The WORKERS begin their rhythmic working with the poles.)

AMERICAN STORYTELLER: From dawn to dusk, seven days a week, the Chinese laid the rails.

CHINESE STORYTELLER: While at night they labored on their secret train.

(The rhythm of their work changes from the drudgery of the day to the anticipation and determination of the night.)

WONG: I have found another piece of silver.

JEONG YUM: And I a nugget of pure gold.

KWAN MING: Our train will be the finest in the world.

WONG: But what shape should it take? It must be different!

FOREMAN: *(Entering.)* Hey. You there. What're you up to?

(The WORKERS return to their normal pattern. KWAN MING comes forward as spokesman.)

KWAN MING: We must work each night as well as each day. There is so much to be done. Don't you agree?

FOREMAN: Uh…sure. Keep it up.

KWAN MING: Yes sir. We will work very hard. *(FOREMAN grumbles offstage.)* Very hard.

(The WORKERS' rhythmic sequence with the poles grows faster and faster. Rhythm increases until finally the Iron Moonhunter is brought to life. The poles now form the supports for the dragon-train, which the ENSEMBLE manipulates around the stage.)

KWAN MING: Toward the moon the dragon rides.

WONG and JEONG YUM: Searching, searching far and wide.

AH DING: Teeth of silver smile at the night.

WONG: Eyes blaze —

WONG and AH DING: And burn —

AH DING, WONG, and JEONG YUM: With fire's light.
    Cross every track, cross every hill

KWAN MING: At midnight when the world is still.

WONG and AH DING: Calling, calling through the night.
    His silver whiskers blinding bright.

AH DING: Sides as red as a shimmering sun.

KWAN MING: He searches for the lost Tong Yun.

KWAN MING and AH DING: From his flutes a call sounds.

AH DING, WONG, and JEONG YUM: Hunting till all lost are found.

ENSEMBLE: Hunting till all lost are found.

(During the dragon's dance, KWAN MING is reunited with his brothers, as are WONG and JEONG YUM. At the end of the poem all freeze.)

AMERICAN STORYTELLER: And late at night —

(The dragon dances again, but this time in a beautiful slow motion.)

AMERICAN STORYTELLER: When you look out across the Sierra Nevadas, when the moon is hangin' in the sky just right, and the wind is howlin' in a certain way, some people say —

CHINESE STORYTELLER: Yes, some people say you can still see the Iron Moonhunter looking for the ghost spirits of the lost Tong Yun.

End of Scene.

Sources

The following monologues, listed by Chapter and cited by character name, were based on characters in my plays listed below.

CHAPTER ONE
Monologues for Young Women

> Aury, *I Got Stories for Days*
> Chase, *What Part Will I Play?*
> Karina, *What Part Will I Play?*
> Elena, "No Room" in *International Holiday*
> Lep, *The Small Poppies*
> Lilly, *Over Here, Over There*
> Kara, *Dancing Solo*
> Tasha, "Tasha's Kwanzaa" in *International Holiday*
> Jasmine, *I Got Stories for Days*
> Meg, *What Part Will I Play?*
> Nannerl, *Prodigy*

CHAPTER TWO
Monologues for Young Men

> Roberto, "No Room" in *International Holiday*
> John, *Over Here, Over There*
> Jackie, *Most Valuable Player*
> Cortez, *The Small Poppies*
> Clint, *The Small Poppies*
> Glaston, *The Reluctant Dragon*

CHAPTER THREE
Monologues for Young Women or Young Men

> Casey/Casey, *I Got Stories for Days*

Cat, *The Sorcerer's Apprentice*
Klaus, *The Sorcerer's Apprentice*

The following scenes, listed by Chapter and cited by number, were adapted from or inspired by scenes in my plays listed below.

CHAPTER FOUR
Scenes for Two Actors

"Boy Talk," *What Part Will I Play?*
"First Impressions," *What Part Will I Play?*
"Talkin' Trash," *Broken Rainbows*
"Facing the Waves," *Surf's Up*
"Impact Zone," *Surf's Up*
"Stand Off," *Blessings*
"The Looking Spot," *Blessings*
"Wasn't He Wearing a Waistcoat?" *Alice*

CHAPTER FIVE
Scenes for Four Actors

"The Game," *Round Pegs, Square Pegs*
"Tea Party in Wonderland," *Alice*

CHAPTER SIX
Scenes for Groups

"The Audition," *What Part Will I Play?*
"To Fly," from "The Woman Who Fell from the Sky" in *Walking the Winds: American Tales.*
"Parents," *What Part Will I Play?*
"The Promise," *La Mascarada de la Vida*
"Ghost Train," from "The Iron Moonhunter" in *Walking the Winds: American Tales.*

Play Bibliography

Blessings The play is available for reading in *Most Valuable Player and Four Other All-Star Plays for Middle and High School Audiences*, published by Smith and Kraus, Inc. Publishers. To order call: 800.895.4331. All inquiries regarding performance rights should be addressed to Mary Hall Surface, 2023 Rosemont Ave. NW, Washington, D.C. 20010. Tel/fax: 202.232.5397.

Broken Rainbows The play is available for reading in *Most Valuable Player and Four Other All-Star Plays for Middle and High School Audiences*, published by Smith and Kraus, Inc. Publishers. To order call: 800.895.4331. All inquiries regarding performance rights should be addressed to Mary Hall Surface, 2023 Rosemont Ave. NW, Washington, D.C. 20010. Tel/fax: 202.232.5397.

Dancing Solo The play is available for reading in *Most Valuable Player and Four Other All-Star Plays for Middle and High School Audiences*, published by Smith and Kraus, Inc. Publishers. To order call: 800.895.4331. And from Dramatic Publishing, 311 Washington St., Woodstock, IL 60098. Phone: 815.338.7170. Fax: 815.338.8981. All inquiries regarding performance rights should be addressed to Dramatic Publishing.

Most Valuable Player The play is available for reading in *Most Valuable Player and Four Other All-Star Plays for Middle and High School Audiences*, published by Smith and Kraus, Inc. Publishers. To order call: 800.895.4331. All inquiries regarding performance rights should be addressed to Gayle Cornelison, California Theatre Center, P. O. Box 2007, Sunnyvale, CA 94087. Phone: 408.245.2978.

Prodigy The play is available for reading in *Most Valuable Player and Four Other All-Star Plays for Middle and High School Audiences*, published by Smith and Kraus, Inc. Publishers. To order call: 800.895.4331. And from Anchorage Press, P.O. Box 8067, New Orleans, LA 70182. Phone: 504.283.8868. Fax: 504. 866.0502. All inquiries regarding performance rights should be addressed to Anchorage Press.

The Reluctant Dragon The play is available for reading and performance rights from Anchorage Press, P.O. Box 8067, New Orleans, LA 70182. Phone: 504.283.8868. Fax: 504.866.0502.

Round Pegs, Square Pegs The play is available for reading and performance rights from New Plays Inc., P.O. Box 5074, Charlottesville, VA 22905. Phone: 804.979.2777. Fax: 804.984.2230.

The Sorcerer's Apprentice The play is available for reading and performance rights from Anchorage Press, P.O. Box 8067, New Orleans, LA 70182. Phone: 504.283.8868. Fax: 504.866.0502.

Walking the Winds: American Tales The play was conceived by Deirdre Kelly Lavrakas. Book and Lyrics by Caleen Sinette Jennings, Mary Hall Surface, and Eric Wilson. Music composed by Deborah Wicks La Puma. Commissioned by the John F. Kennedy Center for the Performing Arts, 1995. The play is available for reading and performance rights through the Kennedy Center. Contact Deirdre Kelly Lavrakas at 202.416.8761 or Kim Peter Kovac at 202.416.8837.

What Part Will I Play? The play published through Encore Performance Publishing, Orem, Utah. All material used herein is used by permission and no public performance may be given in whole or in part without written permission from the publisher. Scenes and monologues for in-class and workshop use is permissible. The play and full performance rights are available from Encore Performance Publishing, P.O. Box 692, Orem, Utah, 84059. Phone: 801.225.0605. Fax: 801.765.0489.

All inquiries regarding reading copies and performance rights for the plays listed below should be addressed to Mary Hall Surface, 2023 Rosemont Ave. NW, Washington, D.C. 20010. Tel/fax: 202.232.5397. MHSurface@aol.com.

Alice
Apollo: to the Moon
I Got Stories for Days
International Holiday
La Mascarada de la Vida
Over Here, Over There
The Small Poppies by David Holman, adapted by Mary Hall Surface
Surf's Up

Acknowledgments

Marisa Smith; Kevin Reese; Bonnie Germann; Gayle Cornelison, Will Huddleston, Shannon Edwards, Clayton Doherty and the California Theatre Center Summer Conservatory Students; Karen Evans and Arena Stage's 2K Playwright's Program; David Ritzer and my students at Benjamin Banneker High School; Deirdre Kelly Lavrakas, the Traveling Young Players, and the Kennedy Center Summer Drama Program; Karen Zacarias, Joanna Lewton, and the Filmore Arts Center; Susan Swarthout and the Smithsonian Summer Drama Camp; Kathy Feineger, Michael Replogle, the Round House Theatre Summer Teen Institute; Harry Bagdasian; Alison Auerbach; Kara Silvestri; Orlin Corey at Anchorage Press; Michael Perry at Encore Publishing; David Holman for *The Small Poppies*, David Surface for co-writing *No Room*; and David Maddox, who helps me find my best ideas. —MHS

MARY HALL SURFACE is an internationally acclaimed playwright, director, and producer of theatre for young audiences and families. Her work has been presented at the Kennedy Center, Seattle Children's Theatre, Louisville's Stage One, Arizona's Childsplay, the Smithsonian, the California Theatre Center and at international festivals in Canada, Sweden, Japan, Scotland, Germany, and France. She lives in Washington, D.C. with actor/designer Kevin Reese and their daughter, Malinda.

131286